"There are two battles we face in every issue. One battle to take ground and another to hold it and occupy the territory (2 Samuel 5:17–25). We all know people who won the battle to get free but lost the battle to stay free. There is a call to fight upon every one of us, and Barbara's book stirs up the warrior that is part of our prophetic identity. Prophets live in the grip of the one true, great territorial Spirit who marked out the land for each tribe to occupy (Judges 15–21). We love the land of the Spirit. We love battle. Barbara's book is for overcomers, warriors and giants: people who want to rise up and occupy till He comes. I heartily recommend it as an important resource in the development of people of substance."

Graham Cooke, author, Prophetic Wisdom

"In *Fighting for Your Prophetic Promises* Barbara Wentroble brings a balanced yet powerful approach regarding hearing the voice of the Lord. This book will be an inspiration to those just beginning their journey into understanding the gifts of the Holy Spirit; it will also challenge those who have operated in the prophetic in past seasons to press into a fresh prophetic dimension in their lives. Readers will receive not only principles for information but also an anointing for impartation to fight to see God's prophetic purposes fulfilled in the earth."

Jane Hamon, senior pastor,
Christian International Family Church,
Santa Rosa Beach, Florida

"Barbara Wentroble has done a marvelous job of providing us with clear guidelines, admonitions, boundaries and, most of all, opportunities to experience the riches and graces of the Spirit's work in our lives, in terms of the many aspects of prophetic ministry. She has brilliantly covered all the ground where concerns have been raised. And without compromising the Scriptures or the intent of God, she has shown us the tremendous significance not only of the role of the prophetic in the twenty-first-century Church, but also of fighting and warring in prayer and declaration for the prophetic utterances, dreams and visions we have received on our journey. May Barbara's work, which you now hold in your hands, serve as the tool she and the Lord intend to keep you moving forward."

Dr. Mark Chironna, Mark Chironna Ministries,
The Master's Touch International Church, Orlando, Florida

"Barbara has penned a powerful tool for all who desire to move in the prophetic gifting and for those who also have received a prophetic word. Readers will be enriched and strengthened in the prophetic. My wife and I have been impacted personally by prophetic words Barbara has spoken over us. Now you as a reader can be impacted as you dive into this book. I highly recommend *Fighting for Your Prophetic Promises.*"

Keith Miller, Stand Firm World Ministries

FIGHTING FOR *Your* PROPHETIC PROMISES

BARBARA WENTROBLE

Chosen

a division of Baker Publishing Group
Minneapolis, Minnesota

Published by Chosen Books
11400 Hampshire Avenue South
Bloomington, MN 55438
www.chosenbooks.com

Chosen Books is a division of
Baker Publishing Group, Grand Rapids, Michigan.

Printed in the United States of America

Library of Congress Cataloging-in-Publication Data
Wentroble, Barbara.
    Fighting for your prophetic promises : receiving, testing, and releasing a prophetic word / Barbara Wentroble ; foreword by Chuck D. Pierce.
      p. cm.
    Includes bibliographical references.
    ISBN 978-0-8007-9513-9 (pbk. : alk. paper)
    1. Prophecy—Christianity. I. Title.
BR115.P8W46 2011
234′13—dc22   2011002963

11   12   13   14   15   16   17   7   6   5   4   3   2   1

There is a young generation arising with strong prophetic giftings. Dale and I are blessed with grandchildren who are part of that powerful generation!

This book is lovingly dedicated to my wonderful grandchildren. May each of them fulfill God's great prophetic destiny for their lives! They make me thankful to be called their "Grandma."

Lindsey Wentroble
Annaliese Wentroble
Anna Kooiman
Gabriella Kooiman
Benjamin Kooiman
Kailee Wentroble
Sylvia Wentroble
Ryland Wentroble

Barbara Wentroble, founder and president of International Breakthrough Ministries (IbM) (www.internationalbreakthrough ministries.org), a strategic alliance for visionary leaders, is a strong apostolic leader, gifted with a powerful prophetic anointing. She ministers with cutting-edge teaching and revelation with a compelling breaker anointing. As Barbara activates giftings and anointings in ministers and business leaders, they are equipped to bring transformation to their areas. Barbara founded Breakthrough Business Network to provide life coaching and spiritual covering for businesses. She also established Breakthrough Reformation Institute (BRI) and Breakthrough Leadership Development (BLD).

Barbara is the author of seven books, including the popular book *Removing the Veil of Deception*. Barbara is a registered nurse, has a B.A. degree from Christian Life School of Theology and a Doctor of Practical Ministry from Wagner Leadership Institute. Barbara and her husband, Dale, reside in Lantana, Texas. They are the parents of three adult children and have eight grandchildren.

CONTENTS

FOREWORD

I know the thoughts that I think toward you, says the
Lord, *thoughts of peace and not of evil, to give you a*
future and a hope.

Jeremiah 29:11, NKJV

Have you ever gotten so caught in a hard place that you wondered if you could escape? Have you ever waited so long for a promise to be manifested that you lost hope? Has God given you a promise that has yet to be fulfilled?

One morning I awoke with the following words ringing through my spirit: *The best is yet ahead. Do not be discouraged by what you see, for I can fulfill that which I have for your life. I will train your hands for war. You will learn to war in a new way with the words I give you. You have a destiny. War with the revelation of My prophetic word until you see Me manifest the best that I intended for your life.*

I knew it was God.

In *Fighting for Your Prophetic Promises,* Barbara Wentroble has captured this concept and created a prototype book to help you enter and fulfill your destiny. When God knit you together in your mother's womb, He had a distinct purpose and timing for your life. He knew before the foundation of the world the time frame for your birth. At the very point of conception, your life cycle—and the beginning of the fulfillment of God's purpose—began.

During our lives we have many choices. Each day when we arise, our first thought should be this: *Choose you this day whom you will serve* (see Joshua 24:15). If we serve God, we will succeed in the redemptive plan for which He created us. We will be aware of His presence. We will know when we deviate from His ultimate plan. We will also know when the enemy of the souls, Satan, attempts to interrupt that life cycle of God. The Creator of the universe has created you and has an incredible plan for your life. Choose today whom you will serve so that your future is assured!

I believe that, as you read this book, you will be able to open your eyes and see God in the circumstances and situations around you. He is Jehovah Jireh, the One who will cause you to realize that your destiny has been provided for and is made complete in Him.

Fighting for Your Prophetic Promises will help you understand the process of prophetic fulfillment. There are many things God has to set in order, or rearrange, before we can see the fruition of His promise. Prophetic fulfillment is often a messy process that seems to interrupt the order of life. Yet even in the midst of drastic change, there is great joy in knowing that we are moving toward God's destiny. My prayer for you as you read this book is that you will experience the joy of prophetic fulfillment in your life.

The best thing about Barbara Wentroble is that she knows God's goodness and can communicate His faith to us so that we catch His heart. God has a future and a hope for us. He has given us promises for salvation, inheritance and spiritual life. Each promise is like a promissory note on which we can base our future. God has every intention of fulfilling it. This is a statement we can take to the bank! It is a sure foundation on which we can confidently stand.

We know God by developing a covenant relationship with Him. From this covenant relationship, we discover God's plan for our destiny. God has many ways of revealing to us His desire for our lives. We may get an "I know that I know" feeling within our hearts. We may encounter circumstances we know have been directed by God that will open or close doors. We may have an urging or intense desire that He is stirring within us—something we know we need to do. We may have supernatural encounters through dreams, visions or miracles. We may be reading the Bible and see a pattern that illuminates something to us in a way that is very appropriate, or we may gain a glimpse of God's destiny for us through prophetic words we receive.

Covenant is key to understanding how to war for our prophetic destiny. God will back you to secure your promises and give you strategies to fight your enemies.

We form a covenant not only with the Lord, but with people in our lives. We must know whom we are to war with. When you are in covenant with someone, that person goes to war with you. I have had a covenant relationship with Barbara and Dale Wentroble for almost twenty years.

No matter what your experience, you have promises from God for a future and a hope. He has a plan and a destiny for you and is working all things together for good to position you so that His plans can be fulfilled. Each time you respond to the Lord in obedience, you see progress in the overall fulfillment of your earthly purpose.

As you learn to war with your prophetic word from God, He will break the power of desolation from you—personally, corporately and territorially.

Hell hates that the God of the universe has chosen to communicate with people. Any time we are getting ready to break forth into a new season of prophetic fulfillment, Satan will oppose us and try to imprison us in the desolation of the past. God, on the other hand, has created each of us to reflect His glory. When we understand our identity in Him and begin to come into the fullness of that identity, His glory is seen through us.

I know of no better book to help you understand that, through the word of the Lord to you, all that God has for you can be manifested in your life. His glory in you will be unlocked as you read this wonderful work.

Chuck D. Pierce, president, Global Spheres, Inc.;
president, Glory of Zion International Ministries, Inc.

ACKNOWLEDGMENTS

Writing this book fulfills a dream that was hidden within my heart for many years. The dream would never have been realized without a wonderful team of other people. They pulled potential out of me that would never have been realized without their help.

Thank you to the following people who made my dream their dream. They also made our corporate dream come true.

My husband, Dale. You stood with me through many long nights as I worked on this book. Never one time did you complain about the time I spent working to meet deadlines.

Our wonderful adult children, Brian Wentroble, Lori Kooiman and Mark Wentroble. Your lives are testimonies to the faithfulness of God.

Our daughters-in-law, Michelle and Britt. I am so thankful that the Lord put you in our family.

Our son-in-law, Brian Kooiman. Your spiritual strength is an inspiration in my life.

Our grandchildren, Lindsey, Annaliese, Kailee, Sylvia, Anna, Gabriella, Benjamin and Ryland. You keep me young and energized.

IbM staff. You believe in me and support me in all that I do.

Executive Network members. Your excitement over this book helped me press toward the finish line.

Jane Campbell, Ann Weinheimer, Tim Peterson and the wonderful staff at Baker Publishing Group. You pull out the best in me.

Norma Anderson. You pored over the manuscript and helped me reach a new level in writing.

Falma Rufus and the IbM Intercessors. Your prayers opened the heavens for me to hear from the Lord as I wrote.

Most of all, thank You, Lord Jesus, for granting me the privilege of representing Your heart on the pages of this book. My prayer is that the book will bring glory to Your glorious name!

Finally, I want to thank the many people who prayed and encouraged me to write this book. This book is your book. Thank you for standing with me. God's prophetic plan for His people is being released in the earth!

1

FIGHTING TO HEAR
THE VOICE OF THE LORD

At the end of the speaker's message that day, she asked for all of us in the audience to close our eyes. I had been enriched by her teaching, and was glad to enter into a time of prayer. At that point in my life I was hungry for spiritual growth; I wanted to grow in the Lord. Thus, when friends invited me to join them for a Christian gathering at a large civic auditorium I gladly accepted. It was a wonderful time of sensing the Lord's presence, but as the large crowd sat quietly, I was certainly not expecting anything supernatural to happen. I had no idea what was going to happen to me that day.

The speaker began to talk in a way that I had never heard before. She began to speak words of knowledge and prophetic words to the people. I was new to the supernatural operations of the Holy Spirit, and did not know about His gifts. I certainly did not understand the purpose of prophetic words. *Prophetic words* are merely the expression of the mind and heart of God in a situation. God wants us to know His good plans for our lives, and wants to help us obtain them. This is why prophecies generally reveal something about the future. This ministry is given to us to help us reach the destiny that God has for us.

The speaker in the meeting did not address anyone specifically with the words she gave. She simply spoke the words aloud, releasing them into the atmosphere. I had never been in a meeting like that before. Nothing anywhere close to this had ever happened in my church!

As I sat quietly, I found myself being pulled in two directions. On the one hand, I had no experiences to relate this to, no way to judge what was happening. On the other hand, I knew somehow that the Lord was at work. Thus, while my mind was fighting to comprehend this unusual scenario, my spirit was also fighting to receive from the Lord. I was truly in a struggle between mind and spirit.

Then it happened. The speaker gave a word of knowledge— information revealed to her by the Holy Spirit that she could not otherwise have known—and then a prophetic word, both of which pierced my thoughts.

"Someone is here today," the woman proclaimed, "who, when you were a little girl, said to the Lord, 'Lord, I will be a missionary for You.'" I barely dared to breathe as she continued. "You will be a missionary for the Lord," she said, "but you will not do it the way that you thought."

I felt as if arrows were plunging into my heart.

Then, as if a word of knowledge and prophetic guidance were not enough for me to try to fathom, I saw a vision. A vision is another part of the prophetic gift that gives a view into the unseen world. The Lord opens your eyes to see beyond the natural and into the supernatural. Through visions, God communicates specific messages.

At the time, I did not even know what to call that experience. I only knew that my spiritual eyes were open, and I was seeing a Sunday school classroom from years past. I seemed to be positioned over the classroom looking down. Inside the room was a little girl who looked as if she was about eight years old. I heard the child, speaking in prayer to the Lord, say these words: "Lord, I will be a missionary for You." Then I knew! That little girl was me. Until that moment, I had totally forgotten about my commitment to the Lord so long ago.

As I drove home from the meeting that day, questions flooded my mind. *How did the speaker know what happened to me when I was young? How did I forget my promise to the Lord? Why did we not have this type of ministry in my church?* I had never received prophetic ministry or words before that day. I certainly had never had visions. But here I was, experiencing all of that within just a few minutes.

But there was an even bigger question: *How could I ever do what the Lord said I would do?*

Fulfillment of those prophetic words He placed in my heart seemed unlikely. Many years had already passed since I had spoken that prayer in Sunday school. I was now an adult. I had a husband and three small children. My idea of a missionary was someone who sold everything he owned and moved to the jungles of Africa. I knew my husband, Dale, would never do that. And he certainly would not allow me to move our children to the jungles of Africa. How could I ever do what I promised the Lord I would do? And what about her words that I would do it *in a way that was different from what I thought.* What did that mean?

Somehow I knew that I would never be the same from that moment on. I also knew that I had much to learn. I had to learn, for instance, to wait for the timing of the Lord. His time and my time are often different. To be in God's will, I also had to prepare through Bible study, prayer and circumstances that would help me shift into God's promise. Without that maturing process, I would not have been properly equipped to receive that promise for my life or function in the Lord's assignment.

That prophetic word changed my life, as I spent years fighting for the fulfillment of His promise to me. It was not always easy. I fought to understand how God could fulfill His word in my life. I fought fearful emotions. I fought unbelief. I fought to learn more concerning God's call on my life. The fight continued until, finally, the prophecy was fulfilled.

Today, I consider myself a missionary for the Lord. I am privileged to minister in many nations of the world. I did not move to the jungles of Africa. In fact, I have made only one trip to Africa, and stayed in a fairly nice hotel. God has fulfilled that prophetic promise in my life, and He did it in a way that was different from the way that I thought He would do it.

What You Will Learn

I meet people regularly who do not understand that fulfillment of a prophetic word from God is not automatic. *If it is a true word from the Lord,* they ask, *won't it simply happen?* Other people receive what they believe is a prophetic word, but wonder: *How do I judge if it is really from the Lord or if it is a false word?* And others ask: *What if I receive a word that seems to be for someone else? Should I share that insight?* And, perhaps most of all, I am asked: *What if I am wrong?*

This book will discuss these and many other questions. The principles taught here will help you step into a new level of *hearing, fighting through and seeing the fulfillment of* God's prophetic promises. It has been written for the purpose of equipping you to receive and to release prophetic promises from the Lord. You will learn how to do battle to bring forth the promises given you through prophetic prayer, dreams and visions. You will learn to distinguish God's voice from other voices trying to sway you. You will discover how people of all ages today are being trained for prophetic ministry.

The latter half of the book will help you to release your prophetic gift. You will be empowered to develop prophetic sensitivity. Prophesying over territories and nations should be part of your prophetic package from the Lord. Some individuals will mature from the gift of prophecy to the office of prophet. Igniting your "fighting spirit" will propel you into your prophetic destiny.

God changed my life. I grew up as a traditional evangelical Christian. Through encounters with the Lord, Bible study and several divine appointments, I came to a new understanding of God's blessings. Through the years, as I moved forward in God's plan, I had many obstacles to overcome. I had to work my way through fears, intimidation and insecurity.

But my life became exciting as I saw the lives of people changed by God's prophetic words to them. I began to experience supernatural visions, prophetic dreams and miraculous healings. You will learn just as I did. And as you see the ways that God has changed my life, you will see that He is changing yours as well.

What Is Prophecy, Anyway?

Looking back on that life-changing experience, I realize that I did not even know what the word *prophecy* meant. Some years later I discovered a group of people who thought of prophecy only in terms of "end-time" pronouncements. They were focused on biblical events that they believed would lead up to the end of the world. That is not our focus in this book. We will be addressing the topic of modern-day prophecy in the context of fighting to hear the voice of the Lord and also fighting to release what He is saying.

Part of the work that the Lord is doing today involves restoring prophets and prophetic ministry to the Church. After centuries of various beliefs regarding prophecy, believers now are seeking truth based upon God's plan for His Church and realizing that a restoration of these truths is needed for the full expression of God's word in our lives. Biblical definitions of the word *prophecy*—the Greek word is *propheteia*—suggest a spoken word that reveals the will of God. The word *prophecy* can also refer to the office of the prophet, as we will see in chapter 9.

One of the places in the Bible where we find the word *prophecy* mentioned is 1 Corinthians 12:10: "To another the effecting of miracles, and to another prophecy, and to another the distinguishing of spirits, to another various kinds of tongues, and to another the interpretation of tongues." The apostle Paul is listing gifts that are given to believers not only during his time but also throughout the centuries, including today.

Prophets can *foretell* or they can *forthtell*. *Foretelling* speaks to us about the future. The Bible says that God sometimes uses prophets to tell us what He plans to do: "Surely the Lord God does nothing unless He reveals His secret counsel to His servants the prophets" (Amos 3:7).

Forthtelling means that prophecy "tells forth" the mind and heart of God. Many people believe that God uses prophecy only in this manner. They do not believe that God also foretells the future through modern-day prophets.

How we need prophetic revelation in the Church today! A glorious destiny is planned for God's Church. Prophets have the responsibility of hearing from the Lord and speaking to God's people concerning His plans. Without this prophetic ministry, we can find ourselves in the same situation as the Israelites in the wilderness.

Moses was a prophet—and was recognized as such. Yet when the people realized that Moses was communicating with God, they did not want to hear what God would speak to them. They asked Moses to be their go-between, to hear from God for them. "They said to Moses, 'Speak to us yourself and we will listen; but let not God speak to us, or we will die'" (Exodus 20:19).

So Moses went up the mountain to hear God's word for His people, and during his absence, those people failed to remember their destiny. They lost the vision of where God was taking them. Since they did not have a prophet in their midst, they moved backward. They behaved the way they saw people acting in Egypt. Scripture records that they engaged in idolatry and all sorts of sin (see Exodus 32). They needed a prophet in their midst to keep them focused on the future God had planned for them.

Prophecy helps keep the Church focused on her destiny. It warns of dangers in times of restoration. Without it, the Church today, likewise, can go backward rather than forward toward her destiny. "When He, the Spirit of truth, comes, He will guide you into all the truth; for He will not speak on His own initiative, but whatever He hears, He will speak; and He will disclose to you what is to come" (John 16:13).

Are All Prophecies from the Lord?

I often say that God gets blamed for saying a lot of things that He never said. An example of this is a story I read recently.

During the historic Latter Rain Movement from 1948 to the 1960s, a move of the Holy Spirit that swept across the world, a spiritually gifted man by the name of William Branham rose to fame. His ministry included the ability to call out descriptions of circumstances and illnesses in people he had never met, which was often followed by miraculous healings. When I say that he could "call out" words, I am referring to prophesying. The minister publicly spoke aloud, or prophesied, what he felt he was hearing from the Lord. Speaking words in this manner is like breathing the life of the Holy Spirit into situations that need His touch.

A minister who attended one of the spectacular services observed firsthand the supernatural operation through Branham. Then, at one point, Branham identified a young lady in the congregation, and described her illness with great accuracy. Branham prophesied that she was healed.

The girl's parents believed that this was a true prophetic word and stopped her medications because of it. The problem was that the girl was not healed. As a result, the girl, no longer taking her medications, suffered from her illness. When they discovered that she was not healed, her parents were greatly embarrassed before their family and friends to whom they had testified about her healing. The minister wrote of his own disappointment and disillusion from the situation.

> Now, some 40 years later, I am still numb telling the story. The accuracy with which Branham described the situation had been uncanny, yet his faith for the healing—or the manner in which the public announcement about the healing had been made—was certainly faulty....
>
> I am an advocate of spiritual gifts and prophecy. Why, then, talk of failure, especially since thousands testified of miraculous signs and miracles during Branham's ministry, and multitudes were converted to Christ? The simple fact is, prophets and prophecies can fail or be wrong.... In spite of stories like the above, I find myself an even stronger (although wiser) advocate of God speaking in our day.[1]

Branham obviously had a true prophetic word in identifying the medical issues—a word of knowledge about the girl's condition. Apparently, however, as sometimes happens in prophetic ministry, the minister did not truly hear the word about healing.

It is possible that word about healing was true, and that the girl and her parents did not know how to fight for it. They may have thought that the fulfillment of the word was automatic. It is also possible that the enemy was placing a trap for the family due to their lack of knowledge in receiving prophecy. They may not have known about the wisdom needed when receiving a prophetic word about healing. They should have had a doctor confirm the healing before discontinuing the medication.

We will probably never know what happened in this situation. We do know that prophetic ministry is a gift from the Lord. We do not want to "throw away the baby with the bathwater." We want to learn and grow so we are able to receive God's wonderful gift for our lives.

I read about another situation where prophecy was used in a wrong way. Several years ago a minister was asked to speak at a reputable venue. The minister was well-known for releasing a healing anointing. The meeting was advertised and about fifteen hundred people attended. He preached a good message based upon the Word of God, and then started to call out words of knowledge, prophecies and words about healings.

At one point, he looked at a group of speech and hearing-impaired people. An interpreter was signing for the group. Suddenly the minister pointed toward them and called out, "All of you are healed!" The interpreter signed the message for them, but no one responded to the call.

Afterward, the group was in confusion, so the leaders of the meeting started to counsel the group. How sad for them to have their hopes raised to a high level but see no manifestation!

What happened? The minister was probably caught up in the emotion of the moment but not flowing in the Holy Spirit.

These stories help us understand a critically important point: We must learn how to judge a true word if we are going to walk into the promises God has for us and see our inheritances come to pass. When you consider further that there are many abuses in the prophetic ministry, and that the enemy lays traps with false prophecies or false prophets, the need for training becomes paramount.

Some people believe that all false prophecy comes from a false prophet, but I disagree. I believe that sometimes a true prophet can give a false prophecy.

I once heard the story of an older man in a congregation who stood and prophesied. "Yeah," the man exhorted, "hath God not written, 'A bird in the hand is worth two in the bush'?"

The organist in the service responded over his microphone. "Nay, God hath not written!"

Obviously, the word released by the older man was not a word from God. That did not make the man who delivered the word a false prophet. He was merely a man who was emotionally inspired and credited something to the Bible that is not in the Bible. He gave a false prophecy but that did not make him a false prophet.

The people in that church had been trained in judging prophecy. They were able to cast aside the prophecy, but not reject the man who gave the word. They realized that he just needed a better foundation in the Bible.

We have entered a new day in which prophets and prophetic ministers are training the Body of Christ for true prophetic ministry. A Christian does not need to reject all prophecy out of fear that some of it might be false. Rather, there are guidelines for judging prophecy, which we will explore fully.

The difference between distinguishing a true prophecy from a false one—allowing us to move forward with confidence—begins with knowing God's voice. The ability to hear and know His voice is part of our inheritance.

True Prophecy Starts with Hearing God's Voice

I remember when the Lord spoke to my heart about the need for hearing His voice. My husband and I were driving to a conference in another state, and we decided to spend a few minutes listening for any instructions or words from the Lord. As loudly as I have ever heard the Lord speak to my spirit, I heard Him speak that day: *Barbara, teach My people to hear My voice.* I knew that I had a mandate from the Lord for my life.

From that day more than twenty years ago, I have taught the Body of Christ to hear the voice of the Lord. It is from that mandate that I feel compelled to write this book. Listening to the voice of the Lord has brought me into a richer and more satisfying way of life. Although I do not always hear perfectly what the Lord is saying, His voice often helps me avoid many of the traps of the enemy. His voice encourages me when my circumstances are discouraging. His voice gives guidance for my life.

I want you to experience the same joy that I have found in hearing and speaking forth the mind and will of God. I want you to experience victory as you discern a true promise from the Lord and fight for it to come forth.

I am so thankful that the Lord still speaks to His people today. I love what my friend Chuck Pierce says about hearing the voice of the Lord:

> Hearing the voice of God is not as difficult as some might think. I have found that many of God's people are hearing

Him, but have not perceived that it is His voice. To perceive means to take hold of, feel, comprehend, grasp mentally, recognize, observe, or become aware of something by discerning. We must learn to perceive God's voice, which will help us understand His will for our lives. Acting upon what we have discerned as His voice until it becomes a reality is the key to a successful Christian life.[2]

God desires for us to know His will for our lives, and we know His will when we hear His voice. Every believer is able to hear the voice of the Lord. Scripture tells us: "My sheep hear My voice, and I know them, and they follow Me" (John 10:27).

It follows that, since we can hear the voice of the Lord, we can also be used by the Lord to prophesy—in fact, we should earnestly desire it. Paul wrote: "Pursue love, yet desire earnestly spiritual gifts, but especially that you may prophesy" (1 Corinthians 14:1). As God reveals His will to us, we must then fight to see His will become a reality.

Questions and Doubts

The Body of Christ has moved forward in this area since I heard my first prophetic word. No longer do we wait for well-known prophets to speak to us. No longer do we limit prophetic ministry to those who are leaders. Prophecy is not bound by geographic location, income, education or age. People in every walk of life have been awakened to a desire to be equipped for prophetic ministry.

My friend Karmen Fierro is an equipper. She is helping a young generation learn how to fight for their prophetic promises. She is equipping them to hear the voice of the Lord and live the abundant life that Jesus promised for His followers. These teens are eager to learn how to hear the voice of the Lord. In most classes she can barely begin teaching before they are asking questions.

"Am I old enough to prophesy?"

"How can I be sure that it is the Lord speaking, and not just me?"

"I'm pretty sure I have a different gift, so can I still prophesy?"

"What do I do if a prophecy doesn't seem to be coming true?"

"What if I get it wrong?"

These teens are not the only ones asking questions. Churches are filled with people who want answers about modern-day prophecy. Some are not even sure that prophecy is still operational in today's Church. Others do not know what they are supposed to do with their prophecies that have not manifested.

These are normal questions and doubts.

My prophetic journey has made me aware of how much we need to hear the Lord's voice. I grew up not knowing that the Lord speaks to His people today. The only promise I was aware of was that if you knew Jesus as Savior, you would someday experience heaven. That is a good promise! But now that I have experienced a deeper walk with the Lord, I have discovered many promises in His Word. I have also received many more promises through prophetic ministry or through hearing His voice.

Some of these promises have been fulfilled; many have not. Just like you, I am on a journey. Not only are we moving toward fulfillment, we are also in a fight today, a spiritual encounter to see the manifestation of everything the Lord has promised His people.

A Multifaceted Struggle

In this battle, we have many skirmishes. As we have seen, we must first of all fight to hear the voice of the Lord. In the next chapter we will look at our fight against the theology of cessationism. That doctrine promotes the belief that prophecy was only for the early Church. It teaches that prophecy has ceased, and is no longer valid for today.

We will also look at the fight for the restoration that God is bringing to the Church. He is helping us understand why we need prophecy in the Body of Christ. We will then learn to anticipate some of the dangers that rise when God restores truth.

The apostle Paul recognized that you and I would experience a fight against the promises that God has for our generation. He penned words that have encouraged believers through the ages to continue to fight until we win the conflict. I love the way *The Message* translates the meaning of Paul's encouragement to us.

> That about wraps it up. God is strong, and he wants you strong. So take everything the Master has set out for you, well-made weapons of the best materials. And put them to use so you will be able to stand up to everything the Devil throws your way. This is no afternoon athletic contest that we'll walk away from and forget about in a couple of hours. This is for keeps, a life-or-death fight to the finish against the Devil and all his angels.
>
> Be prepared. You're up against far more than you can handle on your own. Take all the help you can get, every weapon God has issued, so that when it's all over but the shouting you'll still be on your feet.
>
> *Ephesians 6:10–13, THE MESSAGE*

We are living in a time when God is revealing His heart and plans throughout the earth. He has made a way for His children to fight through every difficult place and be victorious. Allow the Lord to make you a victorious warrior. May He use you in ways you never dreamed possible.

My prayer for you is that you will walk in all that the Lord has promised you. I also pray that the Lord will use you to release

His prophetic promises to those whom He sends you to. Who knows whether you have come to the Kingdom for such a time as this? (see Esther 4:14).

Prayer

Heavenly Father, I thank You for allowing me to be alive at this time. Thank You that I live when You are restoring prophecy and prophetic people to Your Church. My desire is to hear Your voice and embrace the promises You have for my life. Help me not to be distracted or discouraged by unfulfilled prophecies. I set my face like flint to fight against any tactic of the enemy that seeks to hinder me from hearing and obeying Your voice. I choose this day to fight by destroying speculations and every lofty thing raised up against the knowledge of God, and I will take "every thought captive to the obedience of Christ" (2 Corinthians 10:5). Thank You, Lord, that with Your help I will win this fight! In Jesus' name I pray, Amen.

For Further Reflection

1. What was the first prophetic word you remember receiving regarding your life?
2. Has the prophetic word been fulfilled?
3. If not, why do you think it has not happened?
4. What are some of the prophetic promises that you are currently fighting for in your life?
5. What method do you use to take thoughts captive in the midst of your fight?

2

FIGHTING TO ESTABLISH PROPHETIC DOCTRINE

Several years ago a Christian magazine published a story about prophets. The character on the cover representing a prophet looked like a wild man. His unruly hair was blowing in the wind. He had a long nose, and his long fingers were pointing toward the person he was speaking to. The prophet's face was contorted, and he looked angry.

Although the article took a favorable stand toward prophetic ministry, the cover implied something quite different. Most people looking at a picture like that would feel justified in thinking that prophets are angry, judgmental, abrasive individuals.

An even greater number of people do not believe any true prophets exist today. I will never forget the time I spoke to a group at a church during the early days of my ministry. In the midst of teaching, I made an innocent remark. At least I thought it was innocent. This is what I said: "God is restoring prophets and apostles to the Church." I did not elaborate on the topic, thinking everyone knew what I was talking about.

After leaving town, I learned that the pastor called a special congregational meeting for his church to address my "innocent" remark. During that meeting, he made clear to them that no apostles or prophets exist in the Church today. He stated that John the Baptist was the last prophet—and he left no room for discussion.

Among other things, this pastor did not have clear understanding about the position that John the Baptist held. Although we read about John in the New Testament, he was not a New Testament prophet. As the forerunner for Jesus, he was actually the last Old Testament prophet.

After His death, burial and resurrection, Jesus gave gifts to equip the Church for ministry. This was a special kind of gifting, because the gifts are actually people: "He gave some as apostles, and some as prophets, and some as evangelists, and some as pastors and teachers" (Ephesians 4:11). While these people have special gifting, God can also use anyone at any time to give a prophetic word.

Still, most of us, if we think about it, probably conclude that the magazine cover was right. We imagine a prophet—any kind of prophet—to be like John the Baptist—a sort of wild person who ate bugs. What does a New Testament prophet look like?

The New Testament Prophet Today

Mike Bickle, in his book *Growing in the Prophetic*, makes a good distinction between Old Testament prophets and New Testament prophets and prophetic people.

> In the Old Covenant priestly and prophetic ministries: 1) the calling was reserved for a select few; 2) the

requirements were clear and unmistakably defined (the priest's duties were spelled out in detail and the prophets received direct revelation); and 3) the judgment upon them was severe. Prophets were put to death (Deuteronomy 18:18–22) and the priest died in the presence of the Lord if the sacrifice was unacceptable (Leviticus 10:1–3).

The New Covenant is different. The emphasis of Peter's sermon in Acts 2 was that sons and daughters, old men and young men, menservants and maidservants—all were going to prophesy in this New Covenant because of the outpouring of the Spirit. Instead of a limited few, everyone is a priest, and the gift of prophecy is diffused through the entire body.[1]

Like most people who grew up in church in recent decades, I did not know about these gifts from Jesus. We learned that pastors, teachers and evangelists continue in ministry to the present day, but that apostles and prophets ceased after the early Church. I had not attended Bible school at that point in my life, but, actually, many Bible schools and seminaries do not teach that healing, signs, wonders and miracles are for today. In my case, I felt that the leaders knew the Bible better than I did. I never questioned what they said.

Like many others, I was not established in present-day truth. The Bible says, "I will always be ready to remind you of these things, even though you already know them, and have been established in the truth which is present with you" (2 Peter 1:12).

How Important Is Doctrine?

A doctrine is a teaching. Webster's dictionary says that a doctrine is "a theory based on carefully worked out principles and taught or advocated by its adherents." I had agreed with the *theory* of cessationism merely because leaders told me it was true. Later I discovered that the doctrine of cessationism teaches that prophecy and many other spiritual gifts found in the Bible are no longer functioning, nor are they needed, in today's Church.

Establishing doctrines on a foundation of truth is crucial in our churches because doctrines build traditions for God's people to follow. Some doctrines, like the concept of the Trinity—the union of the Father and Son and Holy Ghost as three Persons in one Godhead—are key to our beliefs as Christians. Other doctrines are important to our maturing as people of God and building His Church.

In the book of Titus, the apostle Paul wrote to the apostolic counsels and exhorted them to do what was good. He was concerned about some of the heresy that was in the church on the island of Crete. His instruction to Titus and his leaders was to give good teaching to the various groups. "Speak the things which are fitting for sound doctrine" (Titus 2:1). Sound doctrine demands right thinking and right conduct.

I believe that the Bible clearly teaches—and experience clearly shows—that the gift of prophecy is sound biblical doctrine for today, a key component for building the Church. Prophets and prophetic ministry are not perfect. There are always some dangers involved whenever fresh revelation comes to the Body of Christ. We must be aware of those dangers. Yet, we must not reject what the Lord is doing merely because dangers exist. Fighting for truth concerning prophetic doctrine will help not only those who are open to this ministry, but also those who are hesitant that this gift is for today.

Cessationism: A Doctrine That Blocks the Gifts

After receiving the infilling of the Holy Spirit, I immediately had a deep hunger to know the Word of God. I spent endless hours reading my Bible and praying. One of the things that interested me, as I read, was the ministry of prophets in the early Church. I wondered why I was not seeing it in operation today. It was puzzling because I knew that the Bible says "Jesus Christ is the same yesterday and today and forever" (Hebrews 13:8).

The New Testament teaches that God desires prophecy and supernatural gifts for every generation, not just the early Church.

> Peter said to them, "Repent, and each of you be baptized in the name of Jesus Christ for the forgiveness of your sins; and you will receive the gift of the Holy Spirit. For the promise is for you and your children and for all who are far off, as many as the Lord our God will call to Himself."
>
> *Acts 2:38–39*

I learned later that my church denomination taught the doctrine of cessationism, a belief that was actually curbing the operation of the gifts of the Holy Spirit. Basically, it means that when Jesus ascended into heaven after the resurrection, the supernatural power of God ceased. Just plain stopped! Never mind the fact that Jesus gave the Holy Spirit to dwell in us.

When I opened myself to the teaching of Scripture and saw the truth, I was surprised. How could so many of us be involved with church for years and miss the truth that is taught in the Word of God?

The continuing of the gifts is critical for carrying on the power of God as displayed in the New Testament. Let's look at the main tenets of cessationism to help understand our fight to establish sound prophetic doctrine.

"Miracles Are Not Necessary"

The first argument of cessationists is that miracles were necessary to give credibility to the early apostles who wrote much of the New Testament. After the New Testament was written, miracles were no longer needed since no more Scripture will be written.

Ernest Gentile, who discusses cessationism in his excellent book *Your Sons and Daughters Shall Prophesy*,[2] makes a very good point by stating that Paul would write much of the New Testament, but those who heard him preach did not know about his writings. The epistles of Paul were written toward the end of his life while he was in prison. During his ministry, the power of miracles was evidence of Jesus' authority on earth, and also validated the messages preached about Him.

You and I are also commissioned to tell others about the message of Jesus. We are also equipped to validate this message through signs, wonders and miracles.

> "These signs will accompany those who have believed: in My name they will cast out demons, they will speak with new tongues; they will pick up serpents, and if they drink any deadly poison, it will not hurt them; they will lay hands on the sick, and they will recover."

Mark 16:17–18

This Scripture tells us that any believer can operate in the supernatural ministry of the Holy Spirit. It was not reserved only for the early apostles.

"Prophecy Was Only Valid until Jesus Came"

Another argument of cessationists is that prophecy was only valid until Jesus, who is perfect, came to earth. This refers to 1 Corinthians 13:9–10: "We know in part and we prophesy in part; but when the perfect comes, the partial will be done away." Although there are several theories concerning what the word *perfect* refers to, I believe it speaks of the Second Coming of Jesus. Since He has not come the second time, we still need prophetic ministry.

Some scholars believe that the word *perfect* refers to the completion of the Bible. Although the Bible is complete and perfect, we still need prophecy to comfort and build up the Church, as the New Testament states: "One who prophesies speaks to men for edification and exhortation and consolation" (1 Corinthians 14:3). How we need prophecy to encourage us and strengthen us today!

"The Office of Prophet Is Simply Not Necessary"

Cessationists believe, and, as I mentioned, I was taught, that the offices of prophet and apostle have ceased. Jesus may still give teachers, pastors and evangelists, but those two particular offices are no longer accessible to the Church.

After Jesus' death, burial, resurrection and ascension, He poured out gifts to help His Church mature (see Ephesians 4:11–12). The Body of Christ today needs the fivefold ministry gifts to help us grow up. These ministry gifts, which include prophets, help the Church maintain the correct foundation that was established in the early Church. We need all five of these gifts that were given by Jesus so we can continue growing into the glorious Church that Jesus died for.

Paul wrote about "the equipping of the saints for the work of service, to the building up of the body of Christ" (Ephesians 4:12). You and I can probably agree that the Church has not yet reached the level of maturity that the Lord desires. We need prophets to help us mature into the strong men and women of God that Jesus died for. Prophetic words help people grow by confirming what God is doing in their lives and bringing hope for the future.

"Prophecy Is Extra-Biblical"

This belief of cessationists holds that prophecy adds to or takes away from Scripture. *Extra-biblical* means "outside the Bible." Any prophecies given but not included in the Bible are considered extra-biblical.

We know, however, that during the time of the early Church, prophetic words were given by apostles, prophets and prophetic people that were not included in the canon of Scripture. New Testament prophets were prophesying, but not every prophecy was recorded.

Prophets are not writing a new Bible. Neither are they adding to the Bible. Scripture is very clear that we must not do so:

> I testify to everyone who hears the words of the prophecy of this book: if anyone adds to them, God will add to him the plagues which are written in this book; and if anyone takes away from the words of the book of this prophecy, God will take away his part from the tree of life and from the holy city, which are written in this book.
>
> *Revelation 22:18–19*

While modern-day prophecy is not Scripture, it must agree with Scripture. We will discuss that topic in chapter 5. When the Lord speaks encouragement and strength to His people today, His prophetic words will always agree with the written Word. No true prophecy will add to or take away from the intent of the Bible.

"We Don't Need to Establish a Foundation"

Another belief of cessationists is that apostles and prophets were given in the early Church to establish a strong theological foundation, and that prophets are no longer needed for building a foundation today. And, indeed, Scripture says, "having been built on the foundation of the apostles and prophets, Christ Jesus Himself being the corner stone, in whom the whole building, being fitted together, is growing into a holy temple in the Lord" (Ephesians 2:20–21).

I agree that the foundation of the early Church was established by the apostles of that day. History shows, however, that much of that foundation was lost during the centuries of the Dark Ages.

An example is the message of salvation. The truth concerning salvation had basically been lost until Martin Luther sparked the Protestant Reformation in the 1500s. The Roman Catholic Church at that time was teaching its members that salvation could be earned only through good works. Luther found a verse in the Bible that opened his eyes: "For in it the righteousness of God is revealed from faith to faith; as it is written, 'BUT THE RIGHTEOUS man SHALL LIVE BY FAITH'" (Romans 1:17). A foundational truth of the early Church that had been lost was discovered. Since that time, much foundational truth has been restored. The Church needs a fresh discovery of her foundation in every generation.

"Our Tradition Is Just Fine the Way It Is"

Lack of understanding often leads to rejection of prophetic ministry.

I will never forget the difficulty my husband and I experienced in helping to restore prophetic worship and dance in a church that we pastored. We were living in a very traditional and "religious" area during that time. Although we did a lot of teaching on this topic, some people could not understand the restoration of Davidic worship.

Davidic worship is referring to the type of worship that King David initiated during his reign. David was a worshiper. He instituted prophetic worship at a time when others were engaging in traditional rituals. Even David's wife Michal did not understand his extravagant worship. "It happened as the ark of the LORD came into the city of David that Michal the daughter of Saul looked out of the window and saw King David leaping and dancing before the LORD; and she despised him in her heart" (2 Samuel 6:16). Sometimes those we love the most do not understand our hearts' longing for the Lord's restoration.

During this time that we were attempting to release prophetic worship, we were using banners, dancers and pageantry in some of our worship services. Several people actually accused us of worshiping the banners. One woman told us that Jesus would not allow her to look at the dancers since they were wearing dance shoes. Although some of this may sound extreme, it shows some of the battle associated with restoring prophetic doctrine.

Jesus faced a similar battle when attempting to bring people out of old religious tradition and into present truth.

> "Jerusalem, Jerusalem, who kills the prophets and stones those who are sent to her! How often I wanted to gather your children together, the way a hen gathers her chicks under her wings, and you were unwilling."
>
> *Matthew 23:37*

If Jesus had trouble bringing people out of tradition and into truth, we should not be surprised when we face difficulty in our task.

Dangers in Prophetic Ministry

In spite of objections by cessationists, a fresh move of the Spirit is restoring prophetic ministry to the Church. Still, the Lord is working with human beings, and the potential for error on our part is always present. Here are some dangers we need to guard against.

Danger of Extremes in Prophetic Ministry

With any genuine move of God, there will be groups who move into extremes in their beliefs and practices. In my book *Removing the Veil of Deception*, I wrote about a group that received truth about prophetic worship, yet moved into extreme practices and ended up in deception.

> One of the controversial teachings by the pastor was a series of lectures on "spiritual and soulical relationships." He decreed that the highest form of spiritual realization could be found by dancing at church services with someone else's spouse. Dancing with your "spiritual connection," said the pastor, could open up the possibility of pure spiritual love.
>
> The teachings from this pastor allowed "connected" couples to express the love of Jesus and the unity of the church by putting their spirits together. They were encouraged to hold hands, hug, embrace and even kiss each other. These expressions were deemed proper forms of spiritual expression as long as the motivation was pure.[3]

Extremes in ministry can produce cultic practices. Sometimes exclusive groups develop because they believe they have the latest truth that the Lord is speaking. It is important to remember that God never speaks His truth to only one person or one group.

One easy way to test what we are hearing is to find out what the Lord is saying to other people in the Body. Is He speaking to others the same thing that you perceive He is speaking to you? This helps to confirm God's prophetic word and to keep us from the danger of extremes.

Danger in Lack of Balance

Sometimes ministry leaders who are discerning a true move of the Holy Spirit become so focused on that one topic, they ignore everything else. No one area of restored truth in the Church should put any other foundational doctrines on the back shelf.

In addition, it usually takes a great deal of time for the full revelation of truth to be embraced by those who hear it. If the doctrines of the Church—salvation, baptism, Holy Communion—are forsaken, that body will soon be out of balance.

Only when we continue to balance all truth can we be everything that the Lord intended for His Church.

Danger of Abuse

Another danger in times of restoration is abuse. When the truth of spiritual authority was restored, for instance, some used that knowledge to control the lives of their followers. We continue to hear horror stories of abuse by religious leaders who use the term *spiritual authority* to require blind obedience to their demands.

The prophetic ministry could also be abused by making prophetic promises to those who give money to the prophet. The truth concerning God's blessings of financial gain is an important foundation for believers. There is a danger, however, in using this doctrine for wrong purposes. Bill Hamon warns prophetic people about this in his book *Prophets, Pitfalls and Principles.*

> Some ministries, for example, manufacture "crises" or use guilt manipulation to squeeze donations out of Christians. But we must be above those sorts of questionable tactics. . . . The Bible plainly speaks of a person being specially rewarded for blessing a prophet in the name of a prophet. But when Jesus made this statement He never intended it to be used as a tool for ministers to manipulate people for their own selfish purposes (Matthew 10:41).[4]

Danger of Lack of Anointing

A final danger I want to mention is trying to move forward while lacking anointing. When a fresh move of the Spirit is released, many people experience fresh anointing. After a period of time, God is ready to restore fresh revelation. Some believers do not realize that the Lord has moved on to something new. They try to operate within the principles and doctrines of the last restored truth and, by doing so, lose the fresh flow of God's Spirit.

Some years ago God released what became known as "the River of God," a very real and supernatural manifestation of the Holy Spirit. During the early 1990s, Argentina experienced a fresh outpouring of the Holy Spirit. This powerful move of God's Spirit was also released in Toronto, Canada, in January 1994. Later these revival "fires" occurred in Pensacola, Florida. The outpouring continued to sweep around the world, to many cities and many nations. People experienced laughter, uncontrollable joy and often seemed to be "drunk" in the Spirit. The Body of Christ needed the refreshing presence of the Lord.

When the River of God is released, the power of the Holy Spirit flows like a natural river. We can be swept up into the stream and bear fruit and healing. Revelation 22:1–2 records a vision John the Revelator had of the River of God.

> He showed me a river of the water of life, clear as crystal, coming from the throne of God and of the Lamb, in the middle of its street. On either side of the river was the tree of life, bearing twelve kinds of fruit, yielding its fruit every month; and the leaves of the tree were for the healing of the nations.

When God decides to send forth His revival fires, He doesn't need to ask permission. He just looks for people who are thirsty for the fresh water. "Everyone who drinks of this water will thirst again; but whoever drinks of the water that I will give him shall never thirst; but the water that I will give him will become in him a well of water springing up to eternal life" (John 4:13–14). Many times revival fires and the River of God are like the wind of the Spirit. "The wind blows [breathes] where it wishes and you hear the sound of it, but do not know where it comes from and where it is going; so is everyone who is born of the Spirit" (John 3:8).

A few years after the outpouring of the Holy Spirit in places like Toronto and Pensacola, God began restoring more truth. Some congregations missed this new move and continued to attempt to experience the River of God. They tried to get people to laugh. They made an effort to release the same manifestations they had experienced in the past. It was true that they were operating within valid principles and doctrines God had shown them in the past, but nothing significant was happening. That was because they were attempting to manifest the Holy Spirit's presence in a way they were familiar with, yet without His anointing.

The desire of the Lord is to pour out fresh anointing upon His Church. Today God is forming a new wineskin—a wineskin made up of ordinary believers. He is releasing His fresh anointing on all who will receive, and they will be used to pour out the new wine of revival.

The cry from the hearts of these believers is "The old is not good enough!" Along with the psalmist, they declare, "I have been anointed with fresh oil" (Psalm 92:10). We must fight to receive a fresh anointing for a fresh move of God's Spirit.

Having No Fear

Just because there are potential dangers, we are not justified in rejecting restored truth and a fresh move of God's Spirit. No fresh move is perfect. In fact, it is impossible to have a fresh move of the Spirit without some of the dangers I have mentioned.

There are pastors and leaders who stop prophetic ministry out of fear. Often these churches have experienced confusion over prophecies because they have no sound biblical foundation for them. Sometimes people in their congregations have taken wrong directions as a result of a prophetic word. But the Bible tells us not to forbid prophecy in the Church: "Do not quench the Spirit; do not despise prophetic utterances" (1 Thessalonians 5:20).

Although the Church is in a battle over prophetic doctrine, we are making progress. One of the ways we win this fight is through prophetic prayer (the subject of our next chapter): We hear what the mind and will of God is; we then release His desire through strong prophetic intercession.

This powerful weapon is used to help us fight for our prophetic promises. We also use prophetic prayer to fight for the promises that God made to other people or to various people groups. Don't you love being part of this powerful battle that is advancing the Kingdom of God?

Let's turn now to this very important weapon that we use to fight for our promises.

Prayer

Thank You, Lord, for allowing me to be part of a generation that is experiencing restored truth to Your Church! I ask for Your grace to receive truth that You have reserved for this time. Set me free from any cessationist mindset that keeps me separated from a fresh move of Your Spirit. I choose to embrace restored truth and to reject the dangers associated with it. Alert my spirit when I hear teachings that do not have a biblical foundation. Give me the courage to let go of any "old move" of God and to receive a fresh anointing of Your Spirit. I believe that I receive because I have asked. In Jesus' name I pray, Amen.

For Further Reflection

1. What is a doctrine? Give an example.
2. Define your understanding of cessationism.
3. Describe an area of cessationism that you embraced in the past.
4. What are some dangers in restored truth that you have encountered?
5. Why do we need a fresh anointing?

3

FIGHTING BY THE MEANS OF PROPHETIC PRAYER

Lily Low. Lily Low.

A woman from Texas was preparing for an upcoming conference to be held in Korea where she would serve as an intercessor. For the first time in history, thousands of intercessors were gathering to pray for unreached nations, and also to pray onsite for the speakers and those in attendance. Yet every time she began to pray for various aspects of the conference, the name *Lily Low* surfaced in her thoughts. *Who is Lily Low?* she wondered. Assuming that the Lord had put the name of this unknown individual into her heart for prayer, she was faithful to pray for her. In fact, she battled for her in fervent prayer.

Finally the day came when she arrived at the conference. Out of curiosity she kept glancing at the name tags worn by the attendees when, suddenly, standing before her was a woman named *Lily Low*! She could hardly wait to tell Lily the story of how she had been praying for her, but she was even more astonished to hear Lily's story.

Lily and her pastor husband, Dexter, told this intercessor that they had traveled to the conference in Korea from their home in Malaysia. They were tremendously excited to discover that a person whom they had never met, living on the other side of the world, had been praying for Lily. Why did the Lord have an intercessor pray prophetically and fight for Lily?

Shortly before going to Korea, Lily had become very ill. Her husband had watched, stricken, as she slipped into death. Lily had experienced a stroke due to high blood pressure, and her heart had stopped beating. Feeling a surge of faith, he took authority in the situation and commanded life back into her body. Lily woke, restored to life, but the right side of her body was semi-paralyzed.

Dexter had felt certain that the Lord would send someone to the conference to pray for Lily so that she could receive complete healing. With his assurances, Lily agreed reluctantly to make the long trip.

After meeting this unusual couple, the intercessor sought me out and asked me to pray for Lily. She knew me, and knew that I understood how to fight for victory in intercession. I did so, commanding every assignment of death to be broken from Lily.

By the next morning, Lily looked like a different person. I hardly recognized her. Lily's blood pressure became normal. Her color returned. New energy filled her body. The effect of the stroke disappeared. Now, some twenty years later, Lily is not only still healed and whole, but also fulfilling the ministry that God has called her to.

Praying in Unknown Situations

Why would the Lord ask an intercessor to pray for someone she did not know? How could she pray about things she had no understanding of? Why was it necessary to fight for Lily so that she could fulfill her prophetic destiny? If her husband could raise her from the dead, why couldn't he just pray for her to be healed? If this intercessor had not prayed, would Lily have lived anyway?

So many questions flood our minds when we encounter new situations in prayer. We may never have all the answers, but we do have some understanding about what it means to fight by prophetic prayer.

One of the best ways to activate the prophetic gift is through prayer. Prayer causes our spirits to be sensitive to the voice of the Holy Spirit. Life is full of loud noises and many voices that demand attention. Cars honk horns in city traffic. Children want the attention of their parents. Workers are asking about progress on certain projects. In the midst of so many noises, our spirits can still be sensitive to the Lord's voice. Hearing His voice is critical if we are going to pray according to His will.

A short time after I received the baptism with the Holy Spirit, I was praying for a young woman named Ava. I was not sure how this new empowering was supposed to operate, but found myself saying these words over her: "Lord, You have planned a good future for Ava. She has an anointing to heal the sick. Although she has only seen You do this a few times, the time has come for increase in her ministry." After finishing the prayer, I stepped back and wondered what I had done.

A minister standing nearby while I prayed came to me later and explained how we can pray God's will in situations that we know nothing about. "You were praying prophetically," she said. After a few minutes of talking with this minister, I understood what happened. Rather than praying what I understood with my mind, I had prayed the mind and will of God for the young woman. Although I did not know that she had experienced the healing power of God when she prayed for the sick, the Lord knew. He wanted to encourage her to step out and pray for the sick more often.

Since that day long ago, I have come to realize the importance of praying the desire of the Lord in situations rather than just my own desires. There are times when we may not know the heart of God for a particular situation. And sometimes we do need to pray about the things we understand. Thus the Bible encourages us to pray with the mind and also to pray in the Spirit. "What is the outcome then? I will pray with the spirit and I will pray with the mind also; I will sing with the spirit and I will sing with the mind also" (1 Corinthians 14:15).

God Desires for Us to Pray

The Lord desires for His prophetic promises to manifest. For this to happen, prayer is usually involved. Too often believers think that if they receive a prophecy, it will manifest. They do not understand the fight involved and the necessity of battling through to victory in prayer. In other words, the will of God that is revealed by a word of God is not automatically accomplished.

The Bible records the prayers of Daniel as he focused on the mind and will of God. Daniel knew it was time for the prophetic promise of the Lord to happen. He also knew that God's will for His people was not automatic. Because he understood the necessity of prayer for the prophetic promise of the Lord to manifest, Daniel set his heart to pray.

> In the first year of his reign I, Daniel, observed in the books the number of the years which was revealed as the word of the LORD to Jeremiah the prophet for the completion of the desolations of Jerusalem, namely, seventy years. So I gave my attention to the Lord God to seek Him

by prayer and supplications, with fasting, sackcloth and ashes.

Daniel 9:2–3

Daniel read the word given by the prophet Jeremiah, which told him that God's people would be released from Babylonian captivity at the end of seventy years. After calculating the years that had passed since the release of that prophetic word, Daniel realized it was time for that word to come to pass. He decided, therefore, to enter a season of prayer and fasting, asking God to make His word manifest.

His prayer was established on the covenant promises of God: He knew God would be faithful to keep His word. But Daniel also knew that for God's promise to be fulfilled, he needed to do his part by interceding for the will of God to be released in the earth. Daniel approached God in a spirit of humility, recognizing that God has blessings for those who love and obey Him.

Sometimes We Pray—and Wait

Not only did Daniel know what God had promised His people, he also understood that it was God's time for the promise to be released in the earth. This is not always the case. We do not always know God's timing for His promises.

So many times people grow weary and discouraged while waiting for God's word to be fulfilled. They do not understand why it is taking so long. Like me, they want the promise of the Lord today!

I will never forget the story a friend told me about waiting for her first prophetic promise. Beth was new to the Spirit-filled life, and very excited about the Lord and the move of His Spirit. Her husband, however, was not. In fact, Floyd wanted no part of those "wild" church meetings that his wife enjoyed.

One night, at one of those meetings, Beth received a prophetic word from the minister: "The one you love, the one who walks beside you, will come into all of this in the twinkling of an eye."

Beth could hardly wait to get home that night. She just knew she would find Floyd with hands and voice raised in worship of the Lord. To her surprise, Floyd was not worshiping. He was anxious for his wife to come home. He was tired of sitting home alone, and wanted to know why she had been at church for so many hours.

For weeks and months after that, Beth continued to pray. "Lord, You promised that Floyd would be filled with Your Spirit." The time seemed to drag on forever, and she began to wonder if there was a problem. *Was this a true prophetic word? Did the minister miss hearing the word accurately? Why is it taking so long for God's promise?*

Beth waited for two years. She prayed when she did not see any evidence that God was hearing her prayers. She met with her prayer partners, and asked them to pray with her. She fasted. She prayed for the enemy to be bound from Floyd's life. She did everything she knew to do. Then it happened. Floyd was filled with the Spirit, and began walking with Beth in the ministry God had planned for them.

One day while praying, Beth asked the Lord a question. "I thought You said that Floyd would come into this walk with You in the twinkling of an eye. Why did it take so long?" In her spirit, Beth felt she heard the Lord speak. *Floyd did come into this in the twinkling of an eye. My eye is so big that it takes two years for it to twinkle!* God's time and Beth's time were not the same.

You may have had a similar experience. Sometimes it takes months or maybe years of God's timing for His prophetic promise to come to pass. Do not lose confidence or grow weary during the time of waiting. When we become discouraged and lose faith in God's promise, we find ourselves subject to "hope deferred." "Hope deferred makes the heart sick, but desire fulfilled is a tree of life" (Proverbs 13:12). The word *hope* actually means "to have an expectation." When our expectations are not met, we can become sick in our hearts or our emotions.

It is very important to keep our faith strong during these times of waiting. Reviewing the prophetic promise is like pouring water on dry ground. I like to read the words or, if it is available, listen to a recording of my prophetic promise so that my faith is strengthened. (Sometimes when a prophet is ministering the words are recorded.) The desire for God's promise becomes a tree of life and encourages us during those times of waiting.

Prophetic Prayer Involves Strategic Timing

God has strategic times for His will to be made manifest. The New Testament uses the Greek word *kairos* when speaking of these times, as in this verse: "Therefore repent and return, so that your sins may be wiped away, in order that *times* of refreshing may come from the presence of the Lord" (Acts 3:19, emphasis added).

This word is not referring to a succession of time such as we follow on a calendar; another Greek word is used to describe calendar time. *Kairos* in Acts 3 is referring to a season. It also speaks of a limited time when opportunities are available to do something. The word also carries with it the importance of performing a task, even when it is not convenient to do so. We see from this word that there are times or specific seasons when certain events planned by God can take place. God has a strategic time for each prophetic promise to be fulfilled.

The Bible story of Martha talking with Jesus about her dead brother, Lazarus, is a great example. Martha could not understand why Jesus had not healed her brother. "Martha then said to Jesus, 'Lord, if You had been here, my brother would not have died'" (John 11:21). Martha felt that the time for Jesus to come to her brother was in the past. She felt that the opportunity for his healing was over, and there was no hope for his future. God's time and Martha's time, however, were not the same.

The Bible records that Jesus was touched by the grief of Martha and her sister, Mary, and He wept. I wonder if maybe the weeping Jesus did was due to their unbelief in what He could accomplish. Although her brother was dead, Jesus told Martha that He could still change a hopeless situation if she would believe (see verses 23–26).

After Jesus prayed, He commanded the stone to be rolled away from Lazarus' tomb.

> When He had said these things, He cried out with a loud voice, "Lazarus, come forth." The man who had died came forth, bound hand and foot with wrappings, and his face was wrapped around with a cloth. Jesus said to them, "Unbind him, and let him go."
>
> *John 11:43–44*

Jesus knew the opportune time, the *kairos* time, when He would perform a miracle and cause many to believe. He fought through, or broke through, the circumstance and released God's will in the earth.

"The Breaker" Breaks the Power of Resistance

One of the names the Bible offers for the Lord is "the Breaker." My ministry is named International Breakthrough Ministries. I chose this name because it describes a characteristic of the Lord. "The breaker goes up before them; they break out, pass through the gate and go out by it. So their king goes on before them, and the LORD at their head" (Micah 2:13). He is the Breaker who can break us out of hope deferred—delayed promises—and release His prophetic promise.

Webster's dictionary defines *breakthrough* as "the act, result or place of breaking through against resistance, as in warfare." Warfare praying is sometimes necessary to break the power of the resistance of the enemy and release God's promise. We could think of it like this. When a new discovery is made in the field of science or medicine, we often refer to this finding as a "breakthrough." The discovery breaks the power of resistance to the particular innovation, and releases the medical or scientific community to advance in a new way.

Sir Alexander Fleming made some observations and wrote about the possible benefits of an active ingredient he named "penicillin." He believed the substance could have therapeutic benefits. The discovery did not receive immediate attention. Years later, other scientists took Fleming's findings, and continued to study the substance. Finally, in 1943, penicillin was revealed as the world's most effective antibiotic product. The drug was used to treat soldiers wounded in battle on D-Day in June 1944. The discovery of penicillin was considered a major breakthrough in the field of medicine.

There are times when we are facing resistance against our prophetic promises in the same way that the medical community needed that vital breakthrough against infection and disease. We need God, the Breaker, to break through and advance our prophetic promises.

Receiving Strategy in the Lord's Council

Even when we have the fulfillment of God's prophetic promise for our lives, there can still be a conflict. Satan resists our breakthroughs, and does not give up easily.

David was a man in the Bible who had promises from the Lord. As a young man, David was given a word from God through the prophet Samuel that he would one day become king over all of Israel.

Years passed. Battles were fought by day, and nights were spent fleeing the wrath of Israel's current king, Saul. After much time passed, David was crowned king. He received his prophetic promise. Yet, the promise was still challenged. The Philistines were not happy about David's rise to the throne. They determined to stop David from fully embracing God's promise for his life.

David needed to hear the strategy of God if he was going to hold on to his promise. He sought the counsel of God and obeyed it before he experienced his full breakthrough.

> David inquired of the LORD, saying, "Shall I go up against the Philistines? Will You give them into my hand?"
> And the LORD said to David, "Go up, for I will certainly give the Philistines into your hand." So David came to Baal-perazim and defeated them there; and he said, "The LORD has broken through my enemies before me like the breakthrough of waters." Therefore he named that place Baal-perazim.
>
> *2 Samuel 5:19–20*

David stood in the council of God to receive strategy for his breakthrough. In the Old Testament we find a few individuals that the Lord permitted to be His council members and stand in His presence. They functioned on a temporary basis. "But who has stood in the council of the LORD, that he should see and hear His word? Who has given heed to His word and listened?" (Jeremiah 23:18). This wording refers not only to hearing what God is saying, but also to deliberating with the Lord.

In the New Covenant, God calls more than a few to participate in His council. He wants every believer to enter His presence through prayer and to receive the strategy for breakthrough. You and I are part of the New Covenant priesthood, and have access to God's council.

Joel prophesied in the Old Testament about our participation through the power of the Holy Spirit.

> "It will come about after this that I will pour out My Spirit on all mankind; and your sons and daughters will prophesy, your old men will dream dreams, your young men will see visions. Even on the male and female servants I will pour out My Spirit in those days."
>
> *Joel 2:28–29*

What a blessed generation we are! We are living when the prophetic promise of Joel has been released. You and I have the honor of standing in the council of the Lord in intercession and receiving our needed strategy.

> John the Forerunner was the greatest prophet of the Old Covenant, according to the testimony of Jesus, yet the least in the heavenly kingdom of the New Covenant would be greater than he (Matthew 11:7–14). As a Council member, John was privy to more information than any other prophet ever had been (John 1:33). Living under the Old Covenant, before the veil was torn and heaven reopened, John's access to the Council was limited and partial.
>
> It would not always be so, however. God had given Joel to prophesy that when the New Covenant arrived, everyone would be made full-time Council members.[1]

Although you may not have yet seen the fulfillment of your prophetic promise, do not give up. The Lord has opened His council to you. In prayer we can enter His presence and receive the battle plans for victory.

God also can give us strategy and weapons of warfare through dreams and visions. We will take a look at these powerful encounters with the Lord in the next chapter.

Aren't you thankful that you live during this time in history? The prophets of old could only get a glimpse of what you and I are experiencing as New Covenant believers. We are destined to receive our prophetic promises as we pray and receive the breakthrough God has for us.

Prayer

Thank You, Lord, for the privilege of communing with You in prayer. Help me to get into the right time for the release of Your prophetic promise. I ask that You synchronize my time with Your time. Please open my spiritual ears to hear what You are saying as I pray. Give me the courage to speak forth Your mind and Your heart as I pray.

I command all "hope deferred" to be broken from my life. I will not grow weary as I wait for the Lord's promise. My hope and my faith are in God and His faithfulness to do what He has promised. Thank You, Lord, that I can enter Your council and receive strategy to press through to victory. I believe that because I have asked all of this in Your name I receive. In Jesus' name I pray, Amen.

For Further Reflection

1. Describe a time when you prayed about a situation that you had no prior knowledge about. What happened?
2. How do you pray the mind and will of God rather than your own understanding about a situation?

3. Why is one of the names of the Lord "God of the Breakthrough"?

4. How should a person prevent hope being deferred in his or her life?

5. Why does a person need to participate in God's council?

4

FIGHTING THROUGH PROPHETIC DREAMS AND VISIONS

The dream was still lingering in his mind. It would not go away. Harold was attending a conference on the topic of growing in prophetic gifting, and was puzzled by the dream he had had the night before. Then, his opportunity arrived. "Who has had a recent dream that you do not understand?" Chuck Pierce asked. Chuck and I were leading one of the conference meetings together on the topic of understanding prophetic dreams, and we were including the attendees in our discussion. Immediately Harold's hand went up. This was an answer to prayer for him.

After Harold told the group what he had dreamed, Chuck and I began to interpret the dream for him. Harold was riding a bicycle in the dream. He had painted the bike yellow, but the yellow paint covered only about 75 percent of his bike. The rest was still rusty.

The interpretation of the dream spoke of the restoration that God was doing in Harold's life. The bicycle represented how he was moving forward to his destiny. Yellow is a color that speaks of sunlight and glory. Harold had been allowing the Lord to heal some old wounds in his heart; he truly wanted to be whole and be a good representative of the Lord. The yellow paint symbolized that he had made progress, and was about 75 percent healed. The rusty part of the bike revealed that he still needed more healing, but he had made great progress.

How excited Harold was when the interpretation came! He needed to know that he really was making progress. Even though there was still some rust on the bike, he was encouraged to know that he was further along than he thought.

God's Supernatural Speech

People living in Western cultures often ignore the importance of dreams and visions. They generally believe that valid knowledge can come only from the five senses or from reason. Many Christians in these cultures resist the supernatural, including miracles and gifts of the Spirit. It is a mindset that has been molded by Greek philosophy, which teaches that humans are supreme. This philosophy is called secular humanism.

A Hebrew mindset, on the other hand, sees God as the center of the universe, not humans. Truth, in this view, does not come from human reason but from divine revelation. This biblical view helps us understand that the Lord speaks to prophetically gifted people through both dreams and visions. "Hear now My words: If there is a prophet among you, I, the LORD, shall make Myself known to him in a vision I shall speak with him in a dream" (Numbers 12:6).

The Lord also speaks through dreams and visions to every believer, not just prophets. "'IT SHALL BE IN THE LAST DAYS,' God says, 'that I will pour forth of My Spirit on all mankind; and your sons and your daughters shall prophesy, and your young men shall see visions, and your old men shall dream dreams'" (Acts 2:17).

Dreams and visions are promised from the Lord for His people. They are a powerful means for hearing God speak. They can be revelations that encourage, strengthen, warn of danger or give direction for life. They can be used to reveal our inner conflicts, and also to encourage us along life's journey.

In the same way that God gave Harold a dream to encourage him in his healing process, God gives dreams and visions to reveal His direction and intervention in our lives. We can use them to battle for total victory in achieving our prophetic promises.

The Language of Symbols

I frequently travel to nations that speak a language different from my native English. In those countries I use an interpreter to help me understand what they are saying. I also use an interpreter to communicate my message to the people. In the same way that an interpreter is needed to convey my message into another language, we need to be able to interpret the symbols in dreams and visions in order to receive the messages and wisdom of God for our lives.

Let me mention here that dreams occur when a person is sleeping. Often dreams are used to convey messages to the dreamer that would not be noticed while awake. Visions occur when a person is fully conscious. A vision is actually seeing invisible objects as clearly as if they were visible. A vision is like a picture that is formed when there is nothing physically visible at the moment. It is like a snapshot of something that is invisible but leaves an imprint on our hearts and minds.

God speaks in dreams and visions through the language of symbols. These supernatural messages are often filled with colors, objects or people that are designed to convey a message to us. The bicycle, rust and yellow paint were all symbols in Harold's dream, for instance.

Since dreams and visions are not always literal, they generally show people and circumstances that merely symbolize what the Lord is saying. At times an intercessor has talked to me about a dream regarding a pastor in an adulterous relationship. My counsel and encouragement are that the intercessor not take the dream literally. Rather than coming to a wrong conclusion, a person should pray and ask the Lord to reveal what He is saying. Many leaders have been wrongly accused due to a wrong dream interpretation.

Entire books have been written that give us understanding of symbolic objects, creatures, actions, numbers, colors, directions and places. Teacher and author Kevin J. Conner emphasizes the importance of symbolic interpretation in his book *Interpreting the Symbols and Types.*

> Symbolology and typology are the most neglected fields of study. Types and symbols are regarded by many as of little importance. However, much of the richness of Scripture truth is lost if the believer does not acquaint himself with the language of the type.
>
> God has woven throughout His Books numerous symbols and types, each revealing characteristics and shades of meaning that would be lost to the Bible student were such not there. One cannot understand much of the language of the Bible without understanding of the symbol and the language of the type.[1]

Often God will use objects in dreams and visions that are familiar to the dreamer. Joseph was seventeen years old when he had a prophetic dream. God used objects that Joseph saw in everyday life. He dreamed of binding sheaves of grain in the field, and saw the brothers' sheaves bow down to his. Both Joseph and his brothers understood the message from the dream. "His brothers said to him, 'Are you actually going to reign over us? Or are you really going to rule over us?' So they hated him even more for his dreams and for his words" (Genesis 37:8).

Later in life, God was able to use Joseph's ability to interpret dreams while in Egypt. He understood and explained the dreams of Pharaoh's butler and baker. These dream interpretations provided the fuel needed to release him from prison. His later interpretation of Pharaoh's dream elevated him in power to second-in-command (see Genesis 40–41).

This tells us that interpretation of dreams can be used to speak to unbelieving people. This gift can be instrumental in releasing favor and promotion. Further, it is a powerful weapon of spiritual war in releasing a person into his or her destiny.

Revealing the Enemy's Plans

God often uses dreams to reveal the presence of evil spirits. God wants to alert us to any dangers so that we can break the hold of the enemy in our lives. Jane Hamon wrote about a couple who moved into a house. The woman had had a significant dream several years before that caused her concern in her new home. Jane not only helped the woman discern the interpretation of the dream, but also gave her wisdom in dealing with spirits that were still in the house from the previous owner. The dream contained vital information as to the source of the woman's discomfort.

> [In the dream, the] house had decoration on the walls
> that resembled the images of Eastern gods. As they sat
> at a table together, the gods started moving and causing

demonstrations of occult power throughout the house, affecting all who dwelt in the house. . . .

[Jane learned from the couple that the] previous owners had been deeply involved with Eastern religion and had even left statues and altars in the house when they moved. The couple had had to deal with certain occult manifestations since moving in but had never associated these problems with her dream of years ago or the activities of the home's previous owners. The dream, when properly interpreted, provided the key to dealing with these lingering spiritual powers.[2]

The home that this couple moved into was meant to be a blessing from the Lord. The enemy was attempting to steal their peace and turn their blessing into a curse. God gave a prophetic dream to reveal the enemy. He also gave a battle plan to break the enemy's stronghold that was holding back God's blessings. After cleansing their home from occult powers, the couple was able to enjoy the home that the Lord provided for them.

Responding to Dreams and Visions

We read in the gospels that Joseph was warned by an angel in a dream to take Mary and the baby Jesus to Egypt.

> Now when they had gone, behold, an angel of the Lord appeared to Joseph in a dream and said, "Get up! Take the Child and His mother and flee to Egypt, and remain there until I tell you; for Herod is going to search for the Child to destroy Him."
>
> *Matthew 2:13*

Joseph understood the dream and took Jesus and His mother to Egypt. They remained there until Herod died and it was safe to return home.

It is important not to become fearful when the dream involves danger. A person must discern if action is to be taken, like Joseph bringing his family to Egypt, or if the right action to take is intercession. Every plan of the enemy does not need to occur; prayer can stop it. Intercession is designed to cut off his intended destruction.

A friend of mine dreamed about her son driving a truck. In the dream she saw him fall asleep and the truck veer off the road. She awakened, feeling in her spirit that she had been alerted to pray for her son's safety. After praying, she fell back asleep.

The next morning her son called. He told her how he had fallen asleep at the wheel of his truck and woke up just in time to keep the truck from going off the road. The prophetic dream followed by intercession was used to avoid a major accident and possible death.

Dreams about Death

I remember a dream that our daughter, Lori, had when she was attending a private Christian school. Rules were stringent in that school, and the older children were required to follow the same rules as the younger ones. Lori was struggling with being treated like a first grader now that she was in middle school. She wanted to go back to public school. Lori begged us to transfer her and gave us her reasons. "At some point," she said, "I need to be a responsible Christian and stand up for what I believe." Dale and I agreed with that. Our question was *Is this the time for her to make that move?*

During this time, Lori had a dream. In it, she saw her older brother dying in a coffin. She was trying to get him out, but was unsuccessful. Lori was quite distressed over the dream, and could not understand what it meant. After praying, I felt the Lord gave me the interpretation. Lori had always been mature for her age.

Her older brother represented someone older than she. She was feeling as if she was dying in a confined place. Her vision and goals seemed to be smothered in her current classroom. She felt helpless to change the situation.

After we prayed, Dale and I felt the release to transfer her to a school that would allow her to grow and develop. When she moved to the new school, she was filled with new vision. She was able to be a strong Christian witness among her peers.

How thankful we were for the dream to help us know the will of the Lord in Lori's life! Had we not prayed for revelation from the Lord, we could have missed the true interpretation of the dream. We may have thought that our son was about to die. We could have been engulfed in fear. The interpretation revealed to us the true message from the Lord so we could take the proper action. Parents should always listen to the dreams of their children. God can speak to them, and help them find direction for their lives.

I want to mention, also, that death in a dream can represent many things. Often death does not represent a physical death but death to part of a personality or a psychological death. Do not allow fear to enter when you dream about death. Ask the Lord to help you understand what He is speaking about.

Herman Riffel tells the story of dreaming about his own death.

> Just as seeds do not grow and multiply without death, so I have discovered that there is death in our every stage of maturation. The dream will picture it as the death of either another person or the death of our own selves. If I die in the dream, it usually represents the death of my ego. If another dies in my dream, it represents a different part of me. If I know the person who dies, then I may be able to know what part of me that person represents by his characteristics. If I do not know him, then I must wait and find out through other dreams.[3]

Even dreams about death can be a benefit in our lives. These dreams can help us discover areas of our lives that need to be changed. When we know the parts of our lives that God is dealing with, we can then cooperate with Him. We are able to allow God's transforming Spirit access to every area where He wants to mature us.

Other Sources of Dreams

Not all dreams come from the Lord. They can also originate in our own souls, or be sparked by the enemy. Often I have heard people describe dreams that caused them great fear or concern. One woman told me a recurring dream of snakes that were chasing her. She would wake up terrified. These dreams came from deep within her soul. She was a fearful woman, and lived a life filled with abuse and instability. After she received healing from the Lord in her emotions, the dreams stopped. To this day, she has not had dreams about snakes for more than thirty years.

Nightmares and fearful dreams are rooted in damaged emotions. They come from our deep consciousness. They are messages that are calling us to change. I like the way Barbie Breathitt describes the effect of these negative dreams.

> Nightmares are about things in our lives that we fear. . . . Once we face and confront our fears they will stop haunting us. . . . If unheeded, not only may we continue to suffer from the unpleasantness of a "bad" dream, but we run the risk of perpetuating negativity in our waking life.
>
> Sometimes a nightmare can be a wakeup call from God. Oftentimes when we ignore what God is trying to speak to us through dreams, whether consciously or subconsciously we can experience nightmares.[4]

There are several ways to understand a dream and to discern its source. God wants to communicate His heart to you. He wants to warn you, to release healing and to propel you into your destiny. Here are several steps to take in understanding the source of your dreams.

First, ask God to give you revelation about your dream. He wants to speak to you and encourage you. Next, check your dream with Scripture. God will not speak anything to you that is contrary to His Word. Then, ask spiritually mature friends or leaders to confirm your meaning of the dream. Finally, trust your own feelings about the dream. Give yourself time for full understanding about your dream. God is faithful to bring you the revelation that you need.

Pray for the Interpretation of Dreams and Visions

When the Lord gives us a prophetic dream or vision, we then need the interpretation. We do this by following the steps I have mentioned. We also must fight to receive the revelation and the action plan that God has for us.

A vision that I received many years ago is still sharply visible in my memory. While worshiping the Lord at a conference, I saw a wave from an ocean come onto the land. After a while, the wave receded back to the ocean. Later, another wave, higher than the previous wave, came onto the land. This wave also receded back to the ocean. I watched as wave after wave came onto the shore, and gradually went back out to sea. Finally, the largest wave I have ever seen rose from the ocean. I watched as this huge wave came onto the land. This wave, however, did not pause and go back out to sea. As I watched, the wave circled the globe and covered the nations of the world.

As I stood in the atmosphere of worship, I questioned the Lord about what I had seen. *What did I see? What does this mean?* I knew the Lord was speaking to me but I did not understand what He was saying. As I continued to pray and listen for His voice, the Lord impressed on my spirit that I was seeing previous moves of His Spirit represented by the smaller waves. Each wave was higher than the previous wave. Each wave also carried a measure of increased revelation from the Lord. The enormous wave that I saw represented a coming move of God's Spirit. It would be higher and more powerful than all the previous moves of God's Spirit from the past. This move of God would also carry a corresponding measure of great revelation.

That vision changed my life. The picture remains as bright and visible to me today as it was so many years ago. From that day forth, I have fought for that prophetic vision by praying, waiting in faith and reminding myself of God's promise. This lingering vision keeps me energized when I grow weary. It gives me hope in the midst of every negative circumstance. The vision keeps me focused on a better tomorrow than what the Church is experiencing today. How we need to fight for the fulfillment of the dreams and visions that the Lord sends to us!

Thus far I have been discussing how to fight for the prophetic promise you have been given by God. This is just the beginning! There are new words to be spoken, new promises to be released. And the wonderful news is that God has called *you* to be active in prophetic ministry. Every believer can take part in this God-given gift. You can grow in the ability to hear, test and release prophetic words from God for yourself and others.

In the next chapter you will discover ways to grow in greater sensitivity regarding this wonderful ministry. Get ready to understand how your experiences from the past have prepared you for this time in your life.

Prayer

Thank You, Lord, for revelation to understand the many ways You are speaking to me. Thank You for giving dreams and visions to encourage me and to warn me of danger. Rather than fear associated with certain dreams, I receive faith to resist the plans of the enemy. My desire is to know Your will for my life. I will no longer ignore or reject dreams You send to me. With Your help, I will be prepared to receive the blessings You have for me. Thank You for speaking to me and giving me a vision for my future. In Jesus' name I pray, Amen.

For Further Reflection

1. Describe a recent dream that you had and did not understand.
2. How has your understanding of that dream increased?
3. Describe a vision from the past that still lingers with you.
4. Why is the lingering vision important to you?
5. How can you fight through dreams and visions in a new way that you did not understand in the past?

5

FIGHTING TO ESTABLISH PROPHETIC SENSITIVITY

I hear stories from discouraged people every week. Usually these people are completely devoted to serving the Lord. They live lives according to biblical standards. They are passionate in their pursuit of God. Yet, bad things happen in their lives.

I do not have all the answers that these people ask. Neither do the theologians. Sometimes religious people will try to give faultless formulas for the issues these people are facing. Often these formulas don't work.

Although I might not have the answers these people are seeking, I do have a verse of Scripture that gives me comfort and strength through every difficult situation in life: "We know that God causes all things to work together for good to those who love God, to those who are called according to His purpose" (Romans 8:28). Prophetic sensitivity helps us make sense of these times.

Prophetic People Face Difficulties in Life

Prophetic people have their share of difficulties. These difficulties do not necessarily mean that there is sin in the person's life. It does not even mean that God is judging them, and they are getting what they deserve. Rather than believe that God is causing bad things to happen to them, it is important to see that God helps them overcome their tragedies. "I will lift up my eyes to the mountains; from where shall my help come? My help comes from the LORD, who made heaven and earth" (Psalm 121:1–2).

God is in the mountains, but He is also in the valleys. Mountaintop experiences can be wonderful. These are times when we sense the presence of God. These experiences may include times of worship, receiving a prophetic promise, hearing an encouraging message from a speaker. These times help us feel we are close to God. We can believe that God loves us and wants to speak to us.

Valleys of discouragement are the opposite of mountaintop experiences. These times may include loss, receiving a bad medical diagnosis or an accident. These valleys can cause us to believe that the Lord is withholding His voice from us, or that He has forsaken us.

The truth is that the Lord has an encouraging word for us in whatever experiences we are going through. He wants us to understand that He is both God of the mountains and also God of the valleys (see 1 Kings 20:28). Neither experience changes His desire to speak to us.

There are several factors that can help us develop prophetic sensitivity in the midst of either our mountains or our valleys in life. Here are three key guidelines for helping us fight to establish prophetic sensitivity.

Developing Prophetic Sensitivity through Emotional Wholeness

The first guideline in our fight to develop prophetic sensitivity is to learn to handle our emotions in a healthy way. Healing from the negative valleys of life helps prepare us for greater accuracy in prophetic ministry. It is not so difficult to be sensitive to God's prophetic voice when our emotions are positive. When our emotions are filled with pain and discouragement, however, we can easily misinterpret or miss altogether the prophetic voice of the Lord. Prophetic people must fight against dwelling in negative emotions if they are going to develop prophetic sensitivity.

Frequently we hear reports of church splits, divorce in Christian marriages, drugs, alcohol abuse and immorality among believers. If knowledge of Scripture alone could cure people of wounding, we should be the most healed generation ever to live on the earth. Churches are everywhere. The media provide Christian teaching on a daily basis. Christian bookstores, seminars and Bible studies are available for anyone desiring to learn. Even the increase of counseling sessions has not solved this problem of brokenness. The healing power of the Lord is needed to restore a person to wholeness.

Here are three key biblical principles that help us develop emotional wholeness.

Healing through Forgiveness

One of the most important principles is the ability to forgive. The apostle Paul said that he had a goal he was pressing toward. "Brethren, I do not regard myself as having laid hold of it yet; but one thing I do: forgetting what lies behind and reaching forward to what lies ahead, I press on" (Philippians 3:13–14). Paul was not saying that he was erasing the memory of his past from his brain.

He was saying that he would not allow anything, either good or bad from the past, to keep him from his destiny.

Most of us desire to press on, but we have a difficult time when it comes to forgetting what is behind. For us to be free from the problems and hurts of the past and to be free from the consequences that continue to plague us, we must forgive. It is a decision that a person must make to walk in a higher realm of healing and wholeness.

I read this quote somewhere: "Forgiveness is a lovely idea, until you have something to forgive." I agree! It is easy to talk about forgiveness, but it can be difficult to actually forgive.

There are three levels of forgiveness. The first level is forgiving as a sheer act of the will. Forgiving at this level does not mean a person *feels* forgiveness. The person forgives because Jesus commands us to forgive. The person may need to ask the Lord to help him be able to forgive. God will give us the ability to forgive when our emotions don't want to forgive. We simply ask the Lord to help us make a decision to forgive.

I remember praying with a pastor's wife whose husband had abused her emotionally and physically. The couple had just divorced. When I suggested to the wife that she forgive her former husband, she struggled. She named many reasons why she felt justified in not forgiving him. When she finally grasped the concept of forgiving as an act of her will, she was able to forgive at that level. Later, she was able to forgive at a deeper level and come into greater healing. Forgiving as an act of her will started the process of healing. She was in a battle as she fought with her own will in order to take that step.

The next level of forgiveness is forgiving in order to be forgiven. We are forgiven to the same extent that we are able to forgive others. Jesus taught us to pray these words: "Forgive us our debts, as we also have forgiven our debtors" (Matthew 6:12).

Joyce was having difficulty forgiving her mother for years of abuse. She was a new Christian and wanted to have the life of Christ evident in her own life. People around Joyce noticed the difference Jesus had made in her. Yet, she struggled with the effects of rejection, abuse and manipulation. How could she forgive a mother who treated her with such contempt?

Once Joyce understood what Jesus had done for her, she was able to forgive. Before coming to Jesus, Joyce had lived a life laced with alcohol, immorality and drugs. Jesus had forgiven her for so much! She was also able to understand that her mother had never experienced such love from the Lord. Her mother was a person who was wounded, and who had abused Joyce out of her own wounding and pain.

Because Joyce understood the need for greater forgiveness in her own life, she was able to forgive her mother. She could then stop demanding that her mother be what she wanted her to be. She could hand her mother to the Lord, and allow the Lord to take the place her mother could not fill. As Joyce did this, more healing was released into her life.

The third level of forgiveness is forgiving completely. At this deep level of forgiveness, the emotions are healed. The more deeply a person can forgive, the more the person can receive joy, peace, power and love. This ability to forgive completely and permanently is a major sign of the fruit of healing. The person can then treat the person who hurt him or her as if the incident never occurred. What freedom! It is worth the fight to forgive in order to experience that kind of freedom.

Healing through the Presence of the Lord

The next principle that helps a person come into emotional wholeness is recognizing the Lord's presence in every situation.

That is not always easy. When a person has been physically abused as a child, it may be difficult to recognize that the Lord was present. Since He said that He will never leave us nor forsake us, then He must have been there. If He was present, why did He allow the incident to occur?

I encourage those in that situation to realize that the abuser was limited in what he or she could do. Asking for revelation to see that the Lord protected the person from further damage is vital to the healing process. In all of life's difficult situations, always look for the Lord in the situation. I am often reminded of the horrible trials that Job experienced. God is in our circumstances somewhere. We just need to find Him.

Healing through Hearing the Voice of the Lord

The third principle that brings us into emotional wholeness is learning to listen to the voice of the Lord rather than the other voices that speak to us. Sometimes the voice of circumstances speaks to us. This voice may tell us that we are in a hopeless situation. It may tell us that we are a failure. A bad medical report can tell us that we are going to die. Circumstances can speak so loudly that it may be difficult to tune in to the voice of the Lord.

The voices of other people also vie for attention. The voice of a friend, religious leader or relative speaks loudly to our ears. Often, these people are speaking from their own hurts, emotions or judgments, and their voices may not be speaking truth.

Remember, too, that our emotions can also speak to us. Emotions can tell us that we are rejected. They tell us that we are unloved or abandoned. It is important to listen to what the Lord is saying so that the negative voice of our emotions is silenced.

Only the Lord's voice can bring us truth and wholeness.

Jesus turned to the Jews who had claimed to believe in him. "If you stick with this, living out what I tell you, you are my disciples for sure. Then you will experience for yourselves the truth, and the truth will free you."

John 8:31–32, THE MESSAGE

Developing Prophetic Sensitivity through a Mentor

The second guideline to help us develop prophetic sensitivity is this: Everyone needs a good mentor. No one gets to his or her destiny alone. We need others to help us go where we are willing to go. A good mentor will do that. One of the first steps in enlisting a mentor is to look for a person with whom you have an existing relationship. There should be a mutual attraction between the mentor and the protégé. When the relationship is in place, the Lord can cause the mentoring process to develop in His timing. Be open, vulnerable and attentive as the Lord positions you in a mentoring situation.

My friend Tricia Miller spoke to me recently about how her prophetic gift developed. She said that God put several prophets in her life when she was a young Christian, and she learned how to operate in the prophetic through these relationships. They mentored her without her realizing at the time what was happening. Being around these prophets caused her to sharpen her gift. Today, Tricia is recognized as a prophet of the Lord.

Ask the Lord to put credible prophets and prophetic mentors in your life. They will help you fight to develop prophetic sensitivity.

Choose a Mentor Who Has the Characteristics You Seek

A good mentor should model the characteristics you are looking for. The mentor should not become an idol, of course, but someone you respect and trust to tell you the truth. I have several spiritual ministers whom I consider my "spiritual covering." I always encourage them to tell me truth about myself. My spiritual development depends on my receiving truth from them, rather than expecting them to overlook my weaknesses for the sake of friendship. These are people who care for me and want God's best for my life; therefore, I can trust them to help me get into my destiny.

Find a prophetic mentor who will tell you the truth. This person should be willing to help you make adjustments in your character. Be sure the prophetic mentor loves you and wants God's best for you.

Several years ago I helped to mentor a group of developing prophetic people at my church. When I was out of town one Sunday, one young man in this group gave a strong word of rebuke to the congregation. After returning, I met with this young man. I explained why the word he gave was out of order. He was not a prophet and did not have the authority to rebuke the congregation.

A week later we met with the prophetic group that was being mentored. The young man stood and apologized to the others for what he had done. He then told the group why he was able to receive correction. "Barbara told me that she loved me too much to allow me to get away with doing this. Because she loved me, I could receive what she said." A mentor should love you and want you to develop your prophetic gift.

The apostle Paul was a great mentor. He encouraged his followers to model their lives after his walk with the Lord. "Be imitators of me, just as I also am of Christ" (1 Corinthians 11:1). Mentors are not perfect people, but they should display the character of Christ.

Choose a Mentor Who Is Available

Another characteristic of a good mentor is that he or she should be accessible in times of need. If a mentor is not available when the protégé is in need, what good is he or she as a mentor? That does not mean the protégé should be calling, e-mailing or texting each day. It does mean that there are times when a critical decision needs to be made. There are emergencies. The mentor should be available to give advice or counsel, to confirm direction or action during those times.

Choose a Mentor Who Encourages You

A good mentor should also be an encourager. That person should want the follower to go further in his or her prophetic gift than the mentor has gone. A critical spirit from a mentor will hinder rather than help the person to advance.

The apostle Paul was a person who displayed the heart of a father toward those he was mentoring. Rather than having a critical spirit, he encouraged his followers the way a good father would encourage his children.

> I'm writing as a father to you, my children. I love you and want you to grow up well, not spoiled. There are a lot of people around who can't wait to tell you what you've done wrong, but there aren't many fathers willing to take the time and effort to help you grow up. It was as Jesus helped me proclaim God's Message to you that I became your father. I'm not, you know, asking you to do anything I'm not already doing myself.
>
> *1 Corinthians 4:14–16, THE MESSAGE*

Larry Kreider is founder of a family of churches on six continents and travels extensively training Christian leaders and believers in practical living. He wrote about having a good mentor in his book *Authentic Spiritual Mentoring*.

> Paul knew that in order for the church to grow spiritually, each believer must be in vital relationships with others who had gone down this spiritual road before—otherwise they would be content to do what the "instructors" told them to do rather than learning how to hear God themselves. This was wisdom that could only be learned as they received mentoring from a loving spiritual father.[1]

A good prophetic mentor will, therefore, help you fight to develop and sharpen prophetic sensitivity.

Prophetic Sensitivity through Judging Prophecy

Another principle involved in developing prophetic sensitivity is learning to judge prophecy. The Bible encourages believers to evaluate what they are hearing. Is the message from God's Spirit, or does it come from another spirit—man's spirit or evil spirits? "Beloved, do not believe every spirit, but test the spirits to see whether they are from God, because many false prophets have gone out into the world" (1 John 4:1).

There is a difference between a false prophet and a false prophecy. False prophets are those who prophesy out of their own hearts. They are usually motivated by their own selfish desires and for their own profit. They follow their own spirits and the spirit of the enemy rather than the Spirit of God. A false prophecy is merely a prophetic word spoken that the Lord did not send. False prophets speak false prophecies. Yet, not all false prophecies come from false prophets.

A genuine prophet or prophetic person can speak a false prophecy. The person may be a genuine follower of the Lord but missed what God was saying. Sometimes the person can be spiritually immature or simply failed to discern the word correctly. Additional training or spiritual experience is usually needed to help the person become more sensitive to the Spirit of God.

Judging Prophetic Words by Scripture

There are several ways to test a prophetic word and determine if it is a true prophecy. The first way is to determine if the prophecy agrees with the letter and the spirit of Scripture. God will never speak contrary to His Word. A strong foundation in Scripture helps in judging whether or not the word is from the Lord. It is the plumb line for judging all prophetic utterances.

Judging Words by Who Is Exalted

The next way to judge prophecy is to determine if the message exalts the Lord Jesus and builds up the Church. Beware when the one prophesying draws too much attention to himself. A person does not need to be grandiose or weird, display showmanship or do anything that focuses on the messenger rather than Jesus. God's people need to be built up and encouraged. The Lord Jesus should be glorified. When either of these two ingredients is absent, beware the prophecy.

Judging Whether or Not the Prophecy Brings Hope

Another way to judge prophecy is to check if the prophecy brings hope or condemnation. God loves His people. He does not condemn them and leave them hopeless. "There is hope for your future, declares the LORD" (Jeremiah 31:17). Even when the Lord corrects, He provides a way to be restored. The enemy comes to weigh God's people down with guilt, condemnation and death to the future. How we need true prophetic words that bring life and freedom!

Judging the Compatibility of the Message

The next way to judge prophecy involves words given in a public meeting. Does the word fit with the flow of what God is saying to the Body of Christ? If a person senses a prophetic word from God and it does not seem to fit in with the current way God is moving in a meeting, God might be speaking a word to the person individually and not the entire group. Writing down the prophetic word and meditating on it later can help the person understand what God has for him or her individually. The word may be accurate for the person but inappropriate for the entire group.

Judging the Fruit

Finally, does the person prophesying display the fruit of the Spirit in his or her life? The Bible instructs believers to know and appreciate the character of those who are ministering (see 1 Thessalonians 5:12).

The fact that a prophetic gift is operating through a messenger does not mean that the Lord is endorsing the spokesman's character. The Body of Christ has erred by being enamored with powerful gifts in ministers while at the same time overlooking their character flaws. When that happens, the ministers can fall and do great damage to the Body of Christ. In recent years there have been too many fallen leaders and too much destruction in the lives of God's people. This is not the will of the Lord for His Church!

Give It Time

Prophetic people must fight through all opposition in order to be sensitive to the Spirit of God. Sensitivity does not happen overnight. The process takes time. It means coming into emotional wholeness. It means being willing to allow others to help in the battle. It means developing good judgment of prophecies to see if they are from the Lord. Growing in these areas of sensitivity prepares prophetic people to embrace the fresh outpouring of God's Spirit.

I believe that the world is hungry for a visitation of God. People desire to hear what He is saying to His Church. This desire is not limited to a mature, older generation; a young generation is arising that is passionate in its pursuit of God. We will take a look at this young generation in the next chapter. Get ready to be ignited with the same fire that these young ones are experiencing.

Prayer

Thank You, Lord, for helping me to become sensitive to Your prophetic voice. I recognize that there are places in my emotions that hinder me from hearing what You are saying. I choose to forgive every person, organization or leader that has hurt me. Thank You for pouring Your healing love into every wounded place.

Please direct my steps toward the right mentor for my life. I need someone who will help me go to the next level in my prophetic gifting. I choose to receive from the mentor that You place in my life.

Thank You, Lord, for giving me keen insight in judging prophecy. May Your Spirit cause my spirit to judge prophetic words accurately. I am so grateful to be part of the prophetic move of God in the earth. With Your help I will grow and develop an even greater sensitivity to Your prophetic voice. What a joy to be included in this prophetic generation! In Jesus' name I pray, Amen.

For Further Reflection

1. Describe a time when you sensed the voice of the Lord.
2. Describe a time when you felt God was silent. What did you do?

3. Why is emotional wholeness important in developing prophetic sensitivity?

4. What are the characteristics you are to look for in a prophetic mentor?

5. What are some of the ways to judge prophecy?

6

FIGHTING FOR THE YOUNG PROPHETIC GENERATION

"Would you like to hear what your children prophesied in the next room?" I asked. The look on the faces of the parents was one of incredulity. *The children prophesied?* Most of these parents did not prophesy themselves. How could their young children do that?

Dale and I were pastors of a church at the time. We were training our home cell leaders, and I had volunteered to spend time with their children that night. My heart longed for these children to have an experience in the Lord that would change their lives. The enemy sees their desire for supernatural experiences, and is speaking to them each day through TV, books, music, school and friends. It is his goal to capture them at an early age and use them for his evil purposes. How these young people need to learn to distinguish between the voice of the enemy and the voice of God at an early age!

Cindy Jacobs talks about some of the ways the enemy targets the young generation in her book *Deliver Us from Evil.*

We may not be aware of what is happening to our children, but we only have to turn on the news to know that something very awful is at work. We hear about low test scores, drug addiction, children suing their parents, rampant vandalism, kids shooting kids and much more. This is shocking, considering that we currently have in place one of the most powerful prayer movements in the history of the Church.

Could it be that we have underestimated the power and breadth of the occult as we have sought answers to our nation's problems? Could it be that we have not gone to the root of the problem where the enemy plants the first seeds of magic, superstition and witchcraft in our children?[1]

We are in a fight for this prophetic generation. The Church must focus on these young people and prepare them for their prophetic destiny in God. This was my intent as I gathered these young ones together at the home cell meeting.

During the meeting, I told them about a child in the Bible named Samuel. Like most young people, Samuel needed training in order to recognize the voice of the Lord. Later in life, he became a powerful prophet, and used his expertise to help train others. In fact, he started the first school of prophets in the Bible. Until Samuel came along, prophets merely operated in their own gifting.

After telling the story of Samuel to the children, I asked them to close their eyes. We prayed to bind any voice that would speak to them other than the voice of the Lord. I then told them to listen on the inside to sense anything that the Lord might speak to them. After a few minutes I asked them to tell me what they felt the Lord said to them. I wrote down every response from the children.

The prophetic words were amazing! There is no way these children between the ages of five and ten could have made up their responses. They spoke of angels surrounding their homes for protection, God revealing Himself to a young person in another country, God's plan to restore relationships within their families. Needless to say, I was surprised, but the parents were totally amazed. That evening was a manifestation of the promise given by Joel in the Old Testament.

> It will come about after this that I will pour out My Spirit on all mankind; and your sons and daughters will prophesy, your old men will dream dreams, your young men will see visions.
>
> *Joel 2:28*

Young People Ignite Fires of Revival

The Lord has used young people to lead powerful moves of His Spirit in the past. In one instance, just at the turn of the last century, forty students gathered to pray at Bethel Bible School in Topeka, Kansas. These students wanted the same fire of the Holy Spirit that they read about in the New Testament.

During a watch night service on December 31, 1900, a student named Agnes Ozman asked for prayer. She wanted to receive the Holy Spirit to empower her so she could go to foreign lands as a missionary. While she was receiving prayer, the Holy Spirit fell on her, and she began to speak in other tongues. This was a rare phenomenon for believers at that time. Agnes was so overcome with the Holy Spirit that she could not speak English for three days! A fresh outpouring of the Holy Spirit began in Topeka, Kansas, with that small band of young people.

The Welch Revival, which originated in 1904, was also led by a young person. One night, in the spring of that year, 26-year-old Evan Roberts was awakened from sleep. He had a visitation from God that changed his life. His deep communion with God through this supernatural visitation continued every evening for several months. Evan was later empowered by the Holy Spirit and became a revivalist with a message for the country of Wales. Two years later, in Los Angeles in 1906, the Azusa Street revival was birthed. The revival was led by William Seymour, whose parents had been slaves. Seymour went to Bible school in Houston and met some of those who had experienced speaking in tongues in Topeka. He led a movement characterized by speaking in tongues, falling under the power of God, shouting, singing and other manifestations that seemed radical to that generation. People from around the world gathered at Azusa Street to experience a fresh touch from God.

Known as the Great Awakening, this twentieth-century move of the Holy Spirit birthed hundreds of religious organizations and denominations worldwide. It was the primary catalyst for the spread of Pentecostalism.

The next Great Awakening for the Holy Spirit started in 1948. This move of God included evangelicals, Pentecostals, healing revivals and the Latter Rain Movement that began in Canada. The Latter Rain Movement had an emphasis on healing, prophecy and spiritual gifts.

Revivals during the 1960s and 70s included the Jesus Movement, the charismatic renewal and college campus revivals. People from every denomination received the baptism with the Holy Spirit and spoke in tongues. This allowed ordinary believers to realize they could function frequently in prophecy and the gifts of the Spirit.

Today, it is estimated that charismatics make up 27 percent of all Christians—more than 600 million people. What started in Topeka with a small band of young people who were passionate in their pursuit of the Lord has had an impact on nations and generations throughout the world.

Young People Fight for a Fresh Move

Throughout history, we see that young generations desire a fresh move of the Holy Spirit. They want reality, not just traditional religion. Today, we find many in this young prophetic generation involved with groups such as prayer movements, mission outreaches and The Call, a summons to prayer, fasting, repentance and sacrificial worship. The Call does not advertise bands nor does it promote speakers. The Call is committed to mobilizing three generations, every ethnicity and every denomination in America to join in petitioning God for His undeserved mercy and to return to acts of justice that would satisfy His heart. These young people want to be equipped for their prophetic destiny. They want their lives to be used for God's purpose in the earth.

One organization that began with a vision for young people being used to reach the world is Youth With A Mission. YWAM's founder, Loren Cunningham, was a twenty-year-old college student at the time he received the revelation. He had a "mental movie" of waves of young people that eventually covered the entire world. Through the years, young people by the thousands have become part of YWAM's outreach to the continents of the earth. They are passionate in sharing the Gospel in many different ways. YWAM is one of the largest ministry organizations in the world.

Many people remember a couple of young ladies who received the attention of the world in 2001. Dayna Curry and Heather Mercer left the comforts of their middle-class families to pursue their love for the Afghan people. They were imprisoned by the Taliban in Afghanistan after showing a film about Jesus in a private home. They tell their story in the book *Prisoners of Hope*. Heather shares her passion for helping needy people:

> As my vision about sharing God's love with the poor overseas became clearer, I had begun to pray this way: "Lord,

send me to the hardest place. Send me where others do not want to go—or are afraid to go." I had never been satisfied with the status quo. I never desired to lead what might be considered a normal life. I dreamed about pursuing the unusual and the extraordinary; I desired to live on the edge of impossibilities. Helen Keller once said, "Life is either a daring adventure or nothing."

Further, when I considered the people whose suffering I could help alleviate and the sense of satisfaction I would gain by living for a purpose larger than myself, the sacrifice of my personal comfort and security seemed well worth the risk.[2]

Heather and Dayna are young women who demonstrated powerful courage to pursue God's prophetic purpose for their lives. Although most young people will never experience the terror of an Afghan jail, thousands are willing to sacrifice comfort for God's agenda for their lives. We must help empower them for their call. How do we do that? Here are four ways.

Fighting through Prophecy

The first way to fight for the destiny of a young generation is to prophesy over them. We read in the Old Testament that Jacob prophesied over each of his sons: "Jacob summoned his sons and said, 'Assemble yourselves that I may tell you what will befall you in the days to come'" (Genesis 49:1).

A prophetic word helps our youths know what the Lord has planned for their lives. Too many times the enemy tells them that they are a hopeless generation. These young people are barraged with sounds of violence, defeat and death. The music, movie and Internet cultures offer little else but darkness to them. They are desperate to hear what God has to say. I encourage parents and grandparents to prophesy over their children and grandchildren. If they don't, the enemy will prophesy his plans for them.

If you have children or grandchildren, begin by praying for them. Then listen for the Lord to give you a "word" for them. How they need to be encouraged! Be willing to speak what you feel you have received for them. Do not use religious-sounding words but speak words they can understand. The Lord will be faithful to give you further words as you are obedient to take the first step. You do not need to give them specific calls on their lives such as where they will go to school, whom they will marry, etc. Just let them know that God has a good plan for their lives and will direct their steps as they follow Him.

If you find it difficult to speak words of prophecy, help the young person learn about resources that are available. Some Sunday school curricula, for example, have been written to help young people discover their gifts and callings from the Lord that might lead to their destinies. Although some of this is in the early stages, it is helpful. There is no reason for young people to spend years trying to identify their destiny when resources are available that can help them understand that they have a purpose in God.

Caution When Prophesying over Children

When prophesying over young children, heed a word of caution: Be careful not to get too specific in identifying a call on the child's life. It is not wise, for instance, to tell a child that he will be a preacher when he grows up. The child may have that call, but he might not be ready to hear it. It is possible that specific words could cause children to rebel against God, if they think that God wants them to do something they do not want to do.

I once knew a boy who was about eight years old when people began to give him prophetic words about being a preacher. After hearing these words, he would tell his mother he did not want to do that. He would say, "I want to be a fireman." His mother did not understand the full meaning of the word at that time. She did not have any understanding of marketplace ministry, for instance, and could not help him see that being a preacher did not necessarily mean preaching from a pulpit.

The young boy rebelled during his teen years and became an alcoholic. It took many years before he was willing to turn his life over to the Lord. Did the prophecy have anything to do with his rebellion? Maybe. Maybe not. To be safe, however, it is wise to use caution when prophesying specific calls of God for young people.

Be Careful about Word Choices

A second area to consider when prophesying over children is the use of vocabulary. The messenger should speak in a way that is familiar to them. Vocabulary from the King James Version of the Bible, for instance, or certain religious terms may sound like a foreign language to young people.

Scripture says, "If I speak with the tongues of men and of angels, but do not have love, I have become a noisy gong or a clanging cymbal" (1 Corinthians 13:1). Love does not mean a warm, fuzzy feeling. Love refers to the kinds of words and actions that come from God. This kind of love cares more for others than it does for self. This kind of love is meant to govern the practice of all spiritual gifts including prophecy. God's love, therefore, will give a clear message that the person can understand rather than a religious-sounding message that wows the audience. Love the young generation and prophesy to them a clear word.

Caution in Manner of Delivery

The next area where wisdom is needed in prophesying to children is the manner of delivery used. Loud voices, firm tones, bodily shaking of the prophet or other manifestations can produce fear in children. Fear or apprehension can cause them to miss the word God sends to them. Although these spiritual manifestations may be normal for some believers, they may not be normal for the child.

It is not only possible but appropriate for the prophetic minister to control the manifestations. This will not quench the Holy Spirit. The Bible says that "the spirits of prophets are subject to prophets" (1 Corinthians 14:32). That means that the one giving a prophecy is able to control the delivery and still remain anointed. The goal should always be to help the young person hear what the Lord is saying.

Encourage Accountability from Parents

If someone other than a parent or guardian is giving a prophecy, it is important to have parents or guardians listen to the words being spoken. If they are not in the room with their children at the time, then someone should let them know right away what has occurred. Parents can then help clarify the meaning of the word and encourage the children to understand what it means for them. What a blessing it is for parents and children when they hear a word that brings hope and purpose for the future!

If possible, have someone write down or record digitally the prophetic words that are spoken over children. Parents can use this later to remind the children of God's promises. It also is a word that parents can use as a spiritual weapon to fight for their children during challenging times.

Discern Gifts and Abilities in Young People

The second way to fight for the destiny of young people is to discern the gifts and abilities that God has given them. Sometimes parents attempt to prepare their children for what they, the parents, think their children should do in life. The problem is that their ideas might not be God's ideas!

George's father was a physician. He prepared George to attend the university that he himself had attended. He later helped George get admitted into his own medical school. Throughout these years of education, George struggled. He could pass the courses if he worked very hard. The problem was that he hated that field of study. Nothing in him wanted to be a doctor. He did, however, want the approval of his father. It was not until just prior to graduation from medical school that George took a courageous step: He dropped out of medical school. He joined the military, served as an officer and later had a successful civil career. George finally was free to be the person God made him to be rather than who his dad wanted him to be.

The Bible instructs parents in this area: "Point your kids in the right direction—when they're old they won't be lost" (Proverbs 22:6, THE MESSAGE). The right direction is the direction God has planned for them. Helping children identify their gifting or abilities is a major step in the right direction. The Lord wants children to enjoy the path that He has planned for them. A life filled with frustration and defeat rather than joy is not God's plan. Even the hard places can be places of joy when a person knows he is on the right path.

Parents can help their children find the right path by observing their God-given abilities. These abilities are not limited by gender. Rather than attempting to get a son to do the same things his dad does or a daughter to do the same things her mother is capable of doing, the parents should allow each child to develop his own giftings.

Mike Huckabee wrote his story in his book *A Simple Christmas*.

Part of what makes fatherhood so difficult is Christmas. This is especially true when the little tykes are small and

> Dad is expected to perform the "manly" function of putting their toys together. . . .
>
> I've always been mechanically challenged, and I realized it at an early age, when my jack-of-trades dad tried to teach me the rudiments of being a do-it-yourselfer.[3]

Parents can also help their children grow in their giftings by encouraging them. Rather than speaking negative words, speak positive words of encouragement. Young people respond more to encouragement than they do to critical, negative words.

Help the children to vocalize their own dreams about their future. When they know that you are not going to reject their ideas they will communicate from their hearts. Our daughter was sure that she had a call to be a "Mouseketeer." That was a popular character in a TV program when she was in grade school. Although we never thought that was her call, we watched the programs she created. We applauded her performances. Later, she became the school's drill team captain and won several awards. Today, part of her call is a prophetic worship dancer. Her vision was developing from being a "Mouseketeer" to becoming a prophetic worshiper. Vision is always progressive and takes time to develop.

University statistics reveal that most college students change their majors of study several times before graduation. This is because they are trying to find the right field of study for their careers. Helping children identify their gifts can prevent a lot of detours along life's journey.

Sharing the Baton with the New Generation

The third way to fight for the prophetic gifting and destiny of a new generation is to help these young people develop their gifts by positioning them alongside those more advanced in that gift than they are.

The Bible gives many examples of people who "shared the baton" in life's race. One of these people was Elijah. During a time of famine, Elijah was sent by God to the house of a widow and her son (see 1 Kings 17:9–16). The son later became ill and died. The widow sent for Elijah to come and help. When Elijah arrived, he took the son to his own room upstairs in the widow's home. He then stretched himself out on the boy three times and prayed. The Lord answered the prayer of Elijah and restored life to the young boy.

Elisha was a spiritual son who followed Elijah and had his gifting strengthened. After Elijah's death, Elisha performed a similar miracle. Elisha had prayed and the Lord opened the womb of a Shunammite woman who had shown him hospitality. She then gave birth to a son. Later the boy died, possibly from sunstroke. The mother went to Elisha and urged him to go to her home. There Elisha found the dead body of the young boy lying on his bed. He did the same thing that he had learned from Elijah. He stretched himself out over the boy's body. Then Elisha walked around the room and once more stretched himself over the boy's body. When he did this, the boy sneezed seven times and life came into his body (see 2 Kings 4:32–35). Elijah had shared his baton with Elisha while he was alive. After his death, Elisha was able to use his gifts in the way that Elijah taught him.

There is a transference and activation of gifting when people are willing to share from their own wisdom, knowledge, maturity and experience. The young generation is crying out for these types of relationships.

Fighting through Prayer

The final way to fight for the prophetic destiny of this young generation is through prayer. Pray for the generation as a whole and also for any young people you know to desire God's plan for their lives. Whenever possible pray with young people for God to open their eyes to see His good plan for them.

In a time of battle, Elisha prayed for God to open the eyes of his servant. "Then Elisha prayed and said, 'O LORD, I pray, open his eyes that he may see.' And the LORD opened the servant's eyes and he saw; and behold, the mountain was full of horses and chariots of fire all around Elisha" (2 Kings 6:17). The servant was able to see the spiritual forces God was sending to help them win the victory. He saw a good future rather than one of destruction. Young people need prayer for God to open their eyes to their prophetic destiny.

The Church is in a fight for this young prophetic generation. The enemy wastes no time in targeting the spiritually sensitive ones at an early age. We must surround these young people with a sense of prophetic destiny. Having a vision for their destiny will help them release the prophetic gift God has given them. Fighting to release prophetic gifting in all our lives is the topic of the next chapter.

Aren't you thankful that there is hope for this young generation? Aren't you grateful that the Lord can use you to help them win this fight and obtain the victory for their destiny?

Prayer

Thank You, Lord, for this young generation that You are raising up. Help me know how to encourage them. Give me the wisdom to speak prophetic destiny into their lives. Equip me with the power of Your Spirit to break discouragement and hopelessness from their lives. Cause me to see Your plans for their lives rather than the plans of the enemy. With Your help, I will speak words of life and not death. I will speak words of destiny and not failure.

Thank You for sending young people into my life. Give me the privilege to be used to help release them into their prophetic destinies.

May this generation become a generation of revivalists that will change the world! In Jesus' name I pray, Amen.

For Further Reflection

1. Give an example of a young person in the Bible who was able to prophesy.
2. Discuss some ways young people have been used by the Lord in the past.
3. What are some important guidelines for prophesying over children and youth?
4. What are some of the ways you can help prepare young people for their prophetic destinies?
5. Who is one young person that you can speak destiny to? When will you begin?

7

FIGHTING TO RELEASE YOUR PROPHETIC GIFT

Was that the voice of the Lord or just my own thoughts? My mind was full of questions when I returned to my room that night.

- *How can I be sure that I heard God?*
- *What would happen if the prophetic word I gave to that person was wrong?*
- *Am I spiritually mature enough to release prophetic words?*

I was attending a women's conference and was asked to help pray with people at the end of the service. Teams of two people were assigned to pray for those who came forward for prayer. The leaders felt it was better having two people praying together for each person; together, they could minister in a more powerful way. Although much of what was happening was unfamiliar to me, I agreed to participate, and teamed up with my conference roommate.

I was fairly new to the baptism with the Holy Spirit. Hearing the prophetic voice of the Lord was unfamiliar to me. Yet, as I prayed for the people, I sensed the Lord speaking. As I prayed over each individual, I had an impression in my mind of a Scripture, a picture or a thought that would not go away. I had no prior knowledge of the details that came into my mind. *Could that thought, Scripture or picture be from God?* I wondered. Due to my insecurity in prophetic ministry, I did not verbalize the thoughts, Scriptures or pictures I was sensing. These were very strong impressions, and yet I did not want to release something that might not be from the Lord.

After we returned to our room, my prayer partner and I discussed the time of ministry. I shared some of the things I had heard from the Lord. I had sensed sorrow and abandonment in several of the people. I had sensed family struggles in some. I had sensed a new joy and fresh beginnings for others.

My prayer partner responded by saying she had sensed the same things! We discovered that both of us had been fearful of speaking out. Neither of us was sure that we were hearing the Lord. After we confirmed with each other what we had heard, we literally shouted with excitement. We realized that we had actually heard prophetic words from the Lord!

We did not sleep much that night because of the joy of receiving prophetic insight. We could hardly wait until the service the next morning after which we would again serve as a prayer team. This time, both of us stepped out boldly and spoke the words we were hearing as we prayed for people. It seemed that as we grew in confidence, more and more women began to line up in front of us for prayer. We missed lunch that day due to the long line of people wanting prophetic ministry. It was worth missing lunch for that kind of ministry.

My experience that day changed my life. I realized that God can use anyone who is willing to be used. He is looking for ordinary people to be used in extraordinary ways. Although not everyone is called to be a prophet, all can prophesy. The Bible actually encourages believers to covet the gift of prophecy (see 1 Corinthians 14:39). The Lord encourages us to understand that prophecy is important in the lives of His people. Let's look now at some principles that will help you release your prophetic gift.

Prophecy Bubbles Forth Like a Fountain

The Hebrew word for *prophecy* suggests the picture of something that bubbles forth or gushes like a fountain. This is the word used in 1 Samuel 3:20 that identified Samuel as a prophet: "All Israel from Dan even to Beersheba knew that Samuel was confirmed as a prophet of the LORD."

In the New Testament we find God speaking through His people on a consistent basis. Chuck Pierce emphasizes the importance of prophecy in modern times in his book *When God Speaks.*

> The Holy Spirit's ministry through prophecy did not end in the first century. In many accounts of revival throughout the Church's history, when the Holy Spirit came in power, prophecy broke loose. In fact, one of the signs of the Spirit's presence is prophecy. Through the Holy Spirit, God acts, reveals His will, empowers individuals, and reveals His personal presence. Prophecy is a key element of this process.[1]

Throughout the Bible as well as today, we see that God prophesies through His people. He causes their words to bubble forth for edification, exhortation and comfort (see 1 Corinthians 14:3).

He reveals His mind and will to human beings. They then communicate the message of the Lord to people on earth.

I admire the way Ernest Gentile describes this divine process for receiving a prophetic message from the Lord.

> God is beaming His thoughts down on His people. Explained simply, prophecy occurs when a prophetically inspired person extends his or her faith like a spiritual antenna, receives some divine thoughts of God for that given moment and then speaks them forth by the power of the Holy Spirit to an individual or group for the glory of God.[2]

If you are like most people you will face a battle in order to bring forth the prophetic words that will accomplish God's purpose. Here are several common battlegrounds and help for overcoming.

The Battle in the Mind

The enemy has an all-too-successful ploy against us in this fight to release our prophetic gifts: He will try to convince us we cannot succeed:

- *Other people are blessed but we are not.*
- *We didn't have the right parents.*
- *We don't have the finances.*
- *We don't have enough education.*

If we embrace these or any one of a multitude of other negative thoughts, we will lose our effectiveness. Our minds will keep us locked in past seasons rather than advancing toward our prophetic promises. The negativity will remind us of our failures. It will paint pictures of defeat.

We need fresh God-breathed information in our minds for them to be transformed. "Do not be conformed to this world, but be transformed by the renewing of your mind, so that you may prove what the will of God is, that which is good and acceptable and perfect" (Romans 12:2). When we embrace God's Word, we can turn our minds away from our sense of lack and see God's provision. Truth is then able to help us fight for our promises from the Lord.

As our minds are transformed, we are able to overcome tactics of the enemy. We can then fight with confidence for everything God has promised us. Chuck Pierce writes about the mindset of overcoming in his book *Redeeming the Time*.

> An *overcomer* moves past defeats, past traumas, woundings, mistakes, and failures to gain new strength and venture into the next season with hope. In the midst of darkness, there is light. In the midst of light, there is sound. In the midst of sound, we find His voice. The power of His voice chops down the forest of confusion around us. The power of His voice creates a new path in our wilderness. The power of His voice breaks the waters open and raises our heads above the waves of doubt, grief, and despair towering around us. The power of His voice overcomes any strategy the enemy has developed to hold us captive in his chains of defeat.[3]

Facing Fear and Insecurity

An overcomer also wins the battle against fear and insecurity. Here are some of the most common ways this fear might manifest.

Fighting the Fear of Getting It Wrong

Many people have a fear of missing what God is really telling them when prophesying. How often have I heard someone express this: "I wouldn't want to tell someone that God said something He did not say"?

When we understand the purpose of the gift of prophecy we can move past that fear. The gift of prophecy is for every believer. As we noted, the purpose of the gift is to encourage, strengthen, comfort and build a person up. In other words, this type of prophecy is not meant to give direction, predict the future or correct someone's actions or behavior. The Lord wants all His people encouraged and comforted; therefore, when we prophesy within these boundaries, we are safe from making many mistakes.

If you perceive a Scripture, picture or word that encourages the hearer, you can be fairly sure that it is from God. Move past the fear of missing God, and use your mouth to strengthen the person God sends to you.

Fighting to Overcome the Fear of Man

Another battle to overcome is the fear of others' opinions. This is sometimes called "the fear of man." For many years of my life, I struggled with the idea of speaking to groups of people. My voice would tighten up, and I could not get a sound out of my mouth. During that time, I heard a speaker make a comment that changed everything. She remarked, "You will never walk in the fear of the Lord until you lose the fear of man."

That word went straight to my heart. I had not realized that I was being hindered by the fear of man. That night was a defining moment for me. I made a decision that I would deal with that fear. From that moment on, I fought to obey the Lord. I decided that I would force myself to do what I did not want to do whenever He asked me to.

That fear did not go away immediately. The fight to overcome took years of struggle. Each time I felt my voice tighten I would sense the Lord asking me a question: *Is this the fear of the Lord or is it the fear of man?* I would realize that I had to choose which fear I would yield to. My heart would cry out to the Lord during those times: *Lord, with Your help, I choose the fear of the Lord.*

I would then force myself to do what I did not want to do. I would open my mouth and speak. I did not care if I sounded strange with a quivering voice. If my speaking was pleasing to the Lord, then I would speak. The more I yielded to the fear of the Lord, the less I struggled with the fear of man. Gradually, the fear of man lost control.

I once heard someone say in this regard that a person may have two "dogs." Whichever dog you starve will die. The dog you feed will live. I made a decision during that time to starve the dog called "the fear of man." I would feed the one called "the fear of the Lord."

When I speak of fear in this manner, I am not talking about fear as in terror. This is a deep desire to please a wonderful and loving God. If He wants me to speak, I will speak! Fear and dread do not come from the Lord. He wants us to be free to speak out for Him. "Don't be embarrassed to speak up for our Master" (2 Timothy 1:8, THE MESSAGE).

I no longer struggle with speaking to groups of people. In fact, I love it! The enemy wanted to keep me from God's best for my life. I had to battle to release the prophetic words God sent to me. If you are in this battle, choose to overcome and operate out of the fear of the Lord. Ask the Lord to help you fight past the fear that your word is simple and insignificant. Fight to overcome so that your prophetic voice will be released.

Fighting to Overcome Perfectionism

The next area of fear and insecurity we must overcome is the desire to be perfect. Perfectionism can keep us from the risk of releasing prophecy. Perfectionism refers not to the actions we take but to the false motives that drive us. These motives can be built into us while we are children: "If I don't do this right, I won't be loved." Gradually, this translates into not being loved even by God if we make a mistake. This driving demand fills a person with anxiety.

Perfectionism pressures us to withhold a prophetic word until we are absolutely sure the word is perfect. Now, we should want to try to hear God accurately. We should always strive for excellence in ministry. But if we are slow to move forward in giving prophetic words, we may need to check for a hidden motive of fear that others will see us make a mistake, that everything we do has to make a positive impression on people. Perfectionism is closely aligned with the fear of man.

Fight to release your prophetic gift, even if you do make a mistake or two. I will never forget what the Lord spoke to me during my fight with perfectionism. God said to my heart, *I am bigger than your mistakes.*

Wow! What freedom those words brought me! The Lord was assuring me that if I would trust Him, He was big enough to fix whatever mistakes I made. I could trust His love and acceptance even when I did something wrong. His unconditional love set me free in my fight with perfectionism.

I later realized that we can continue to suppress inner feelings or desires until we become an empty shell. Only by receiving God's unconditional love can we be free to be the people we really are. God's unconditional love and His abundant life are available for all His children. Only Jesus was perfect. If we were perfect, we would not need a Savior. This fact helped me love Him more and be willing to fight with any area of perfectionism in my life.

Fighting to Overcome Legalism

The final fear and insecurity that I will mention is legalism. *Legalism* is not a word that is found in the Bible, but the Pharisees were good examples of it, by following the letter of the law rather than the spirit. Legalism requires people to follow a strict list of doctrinal rules and regulations.

As God's people, we must live our lives with care not to accept heresy or unscriptural lifestyles. Yet, we simply cannot allow ourselves to be bound by religious rules that steal the joy in serving the Lord.

> So, then, if with Christ you've put all that pretentious and infantile religion behind you, why do you let yourselves be bullied by it? "Don't touch this! Don't taste that! Don't go near this!" Do you think things that are here today and gone tomorrow are worth that kind of attention? Such things sound impressive if said in a deep enough voice. They even give the illusion of being pious and humble and ascetic. But they're just another way of showing off, making yourselves look important.
>
> *Colossians 2:20–23, THE MESSAGE*

You may not prophesy exactly the way another person does. God made you special and wants to use you in your unique way. Fight past legalism and receive God's grace to release your prophetic gift.

Overcoming a Mindset of Limitations

Next, we may need to battle past a mindset of limitations in order to release our prophetic gifts. People sometimes feel limited by the lack of finances, by their family backgrounds or by their own pasts. People often feel limited by their educational backgrounds.

They may not have had the opportunity to attend Bible school or complete some other formal education.

I am a member of a group of about twenty ministry leaders called Eagles Vision Apostolic Team headed by C. Peter Wagner. At one meeting Peter asked how many seminary graduates were in the group. Only one person fit that category. The people in this group had all reached the conclusion that we would not let educational or any other limitations stop us from accepting the call of God on our lives. We are going to step out boldly to fulfill our work for the Kingdom.

Education is important. We need to be educated in biblical truth. We need much of the education available through colleges and special schools. But the limits of a background devoid of formal education do not prevent anyone from being used by God in prophetic ministry.

Amos was a prophet in the Old Testament, and he was a lowly shepherd. He spoke against those who took advantage of the poor. He also spoke against the religious corruption and the sickness in society. Amos never claimed to be a professional prophet; he said he was serving only because God sent him with a message. Amos refused to allow the limitation of not having any ministry education prevent him from prophesying. Like Amos of old, we must fight past any limitation that will hinder the release of the prophetic gift from God.

Prophecy is only released by faith. "Since we have gifts that differ according to the grace given to us, each of us is to exercise them accordingly: if prophecy, according to the proportion of his faith" (Romans 12:6). Faith grows as the prophetic gift is exercised. You might be able to prophesy only a word or two when you begin. Later, as your faith is strengthened, you may find that you prophesy a paragraph or even an entire page of words. Don't let perceived limitations hold you back from grow-ing in this gift.

Fighting to Discern Prophetic Words

After fighting to overcome negative thoughts, fears and limited mindsets, you might still question how you can know that the Lord has called you to give a prophetic word. Here are several ways to help you determine that you have, in fact, heard a word from God that He wants you to claim as your own promise or share with someone else.

An Inner Knowing

The most frequent way that God gives a prophetic word is by an inner knowing. You might sense a gentle nudging from the Lord, receive a strong impression or have a clearly expressed thought form in your mind. As you hold onto that inner prompting, the Lord will often confirm it.

The prophet Elijah was a bold speaker who was used to per-forming awesome demonstrations of God's power. He had dried up the rain in his country, called fire down from heaven and killed hundreds of false prophets. Later, hidden away in a cave from the murderous rage of Queen Jezebel, Elijah heard God speak to him. God sent an earthquake, a strong wind and fire. Yet Elijah realized that God was not speaking in any of those loud noises. God then spoke to Elijah in his inner being like a gentle breeze. Through that gentle inner knowing, God once again confirmed Elijah's call (see 1 Kings 19).

Dreams and Visions

As we have noted, God often gives words through dreams and visions. Jacob's son Joseph dreamed that he was in a place of leadership, and that in the days ahead his family would serve him (see Genesis 37:5–11). This order was not normal for families during that time. He was a younger brother, and usually the younger brother would serve the older brother. His dream was used to confirm God's call on his life.

We looked at the place of symbols in dreams and visions in chapter 4. If you think you have been given a word through this means, check with mature ministry leaders about your dream or vision.

Scripture Confirmations

Another way God gives prophetic words is through Scripture. There might be a time when you are reading the Bible, and a few lines seem to leap off the page and grab your heart. You cannot forget the Scripture. Its revelation seems to burn within you.

This is what happened on the road to Emmaus when Jesus explained the Scriptures concerning Himself. "They said to one another, 'Were not our hearts burning within us while He was speaking to us on the road, while He was explaining the Scriptures to us?'" (Luke 24:32). They sensed a divine flow of God's Spirit into their innermost beings.

An Audible Voice

A rare way that the Lord speaks is by His audible voice. I am not sure if I have ever heard the audible voice of the Lord, but there have been times when His voice has been so clear that it seemed audible. I could quote the exact words I was hearing. Prophets in the Old Testament often heard the audible voice of God. Isaiah saw a vision and also heard the voice of the Lord calling him (see Isaiah 6).

Although the audible voice of God is rare, it does sometimes happen. My friend Neil Mendenhall recently was awakened from sleep by God's voice. Like young Samuel in the Old Testament (see 1 Samuel 3:1–10), Neil did not recognize it at first. He thought perhaps his wife had called his name, but saw that she was sleeping soundly.

Once again he heard it: *Neil.* Finally, he realized God was speaking to him. The Lord gave Neil instructions on what he needed to do to deal with an offense someone had against him. After Neil followed the directions of the Lord, the offense was forgiven. Great joy flooded Neil's heart. He had not realized that he had caused an offense until the Lord revealed it to him. God chooses how He wants to communicate with His people. Sometimes He chooses to speak audibly.

The Affirmation of Others

As you grow in the ability to hear and speak prophetic words, others will likely begin to recognize and affirm it. Their words of encouragement will help strengthen your resolve to allow the Lord's prophetic gift to flow through you. You will embrace assurance from the Lord that you have been called to be used by God in prophetic ministry. I sometimes say that we can know in our "knower." Our knower is my way of referring to our spirit. "These things I have written to you who believe in the name of the Son of God, so that you may know that you have eternal life" (1 John 5:13). You can know that God wants to guide you in the use of this wonderful ministry.

You may have experienced several of these types of expressions of God's voice, or none of them. You may simply find yourself being used by God in prophetic ministry. Do not allow doubts to hinder you from releasing your prophetic gift. Fight to fulfill God's call and see Him use you in ways you never dreamed possible.

Protocol for Releasing Prophetic Words

The next step in releasing your prophetic gift is to know the protocol for the particular place where you are prophesying. Prophetic protocol is the accepted etiquette or predetermined format for delivering a prophetic message. If the occasion is public ministry, such as a church setting or conference, the leaders of the particular organization will generally have established certain guidelines. Some leaders ask the person speaking to come to a microphone at the front. Others may want the person prophesying to stand and give the message from his or her seat. Some churches require membership classes or other criteria before giving a prophetic word so that church leaders are well acquainted with the person speaking.

A woman came to me during a church service several years ago very upset because the leadership would not allow her to speak prophetically to the entire church. She told me that before delivering a prophetic word, they wanted her to speak the word to one of the leaders. The leaders would then decide whether or not it was an appropriate word for the congregation. She told me that she was allowed to prophesy freely in every other church she had ever attended.

I explained to her that this church was not one and the same as "every other church" she had attended. This church's leaders had a different protocol, and if she wanted to bring forth a prophetic word, she needed to respect their wishes and make an appointment. She could then learn the protocol for releasing prophecy in this particular church.

The woman continued to argue with me that she had always been able to prophesy in every church she had attended. I continued to remind her that she was in this particular church and not in the other churches she had attended. She needed to know the protocol for *this* church. I don't remember ever seeing her again. She probably never returned since she could not prophesy when she wanted and in the way she wanted.

Protocol keeps order in the church and allows the Spirit of God to flow in a way that can be received by those being ministered to. Always understand the protocol for public ministry situations.

If you have a word in a private conversation with someone, again understand the importance of protocol. For instance, you might ask the individual if you may share the message that you have heard from the Lord. I always try to get permission from the individual before releasing a word. I also like to have another family member hear what I am prophesying. These individuals are able to remember some of the details of the word. They may also want to write down the words so they are not forgotten.

As you learn to develop your prophetic gifting, you will likely go through a process of personal growth. The gift is given in a moment but maturity takes time—maturity of both the gift and your character. We will take a look at this process in the next chapter. Your prophetic journey has just begun. What an exciting life the Lord has planned for you!

Prayer

Thank You, Lord, for allowing me to be part of this prophetic generation. I am thankful that You are calling Your people to prophetic ministry today. Help me to recognize the call on my life. I resist every fear and insecurity that has been designed to hinder my call. I break the power of the fear of man. I choose to walk in the fear of the Lord. I resist every limitation that seeks to keep me from God's plan for my life.

With Your grace, I fight to embrace my call. With Your help I will step out in faith and prophesy Your word. Thank You, Lord, for releasing Your prophetic gift through me. In Jesus' name I pray, Amen.

For Further Reflection

1. Describe a time when you sensed the Lord was giving you a prophetic word. What did you do?
2. What are some of the fears and insecurities that you have experienced in your life? How did you deal with them?
3. What is prophetic protocol?
4. How might God give a prophetic word?
5. Do you accept your call to prophetic ministry?

8

FIGHTING TO DEVELOP YOUR PROPHETIC GIFT

How excited five-year-old Abby was when she came home from school that day! She held in her hand a container with potting soil. She had planted a small seed in the soil and had been given instructions to water the seed each day. Within a few weeks, she was told, the seed should begin to grow and form a plant. By summer, if she was faithful to follow the directions, a beautiful flower would appear. Abby could hardly wait for the promise of the flower.

Over those next few weeks, challenges came. There were days when Abby forgot to water her seed. There were times when the tiny plant did not look as if it would survive until summer. Day after day she persevered, wondering if she would ever see her beautiful flower.

This little girl's adventure is a good description of the battle you and I face in order to see God's prophetic promises realized in our lives, as well as learn to receive and give those promises. There are days when we are not faithful to do everything we know that we should do. There are times when it seems that our prophetic word is not growing the way it should grow. It can also seem to take forever for our gift to develop into its full potential.

Not long ago I was given a digital photo frame, which is designed to give a slide show of pictures as well as the time and date. *What a wonderful way to see my grandchildren's pictures as I work!* I thought.

It looked so simple. Yet after several days of reading instructions and changing various settings, I still could not get that piece of equipment to work the way I was told it should function. How frustrating! I was excited to receive the gift, but did not know there would be such a battle to learn to operate it. Finally after several more days of struggle, I was able to get the photos, clock and calendar all synchronized.

Just so with the prophetic gifting in our lives. For it to function the way it is designed to function, we need to fight to develop it. Don't give up. Understanding the process will help you press through the battle to mature your gift and your character.

And, by the way, Abby's flower bloomed beautifully.

The Four Realms of Prophecy

The process begins with understanding the four particular realms of prophecy. Webster's defines the word *realm* as a "field, sphere or domain." These realms together give a complete picture of the functions and limitations of the different aspects of prophetic ministry.

The Prophecy of Scripture

The first realm of prophecy to understand is that the Bible itself is a prophetic work (see 2 Peter 1:20–21). Scripture is the highest form of prophecy; all prophecy must be judged by it. The first question to ask, then, when you receive a word of prophecy is this: Does this prophecy agree with both the letter and the spirit of Scripture?

The Lord may also give you a portion of Scripture that is itself a prophetic word to guide you. There are several ways He could do this. A friend might mention a verse that has a particular meaning. You might "happen" to read a verse that speaks specifically to your situation. A verse that you have not thought of for some time might come to mind.

After receiving the baptism with the Holy Spirit, I was asked to lead a Christian women's organization. I was both new to the organization and unsure about the operation of the spiritual gifts.

In prayer, I asked the Lord to speak to me. I wanted to know if I should accept the assignment. Somewhere inside of me I sensed the impression of a verse that, actually, did not seem to fit the situation: "Be diligent to present yourself approved to God as a workman who does not need to be ashamed, accurately handling the word of truth" (2 Timothy 2:15).

I wanted to know if I should lead the organization, and the Lord responded by guiding me to study His Word. Little did I know how important that verse would be to me in the days ahead. It was indeed a prophetic word.

I sensed the approval of God to lead the organization. At the same time, I submerged myself in prayer and the Word of God. The organization grew beyond my expectations. I used the verse given me about being a workman that is not ashamed to battle through difficult decisions and handle hard situations. God put a weapon in my hand in the form of Scripture. That verse strengthened me in times when I was unsure of my ability to lead the organization. I needed to fight with that weapon to be successful as a prophetic leader.

The Gift of Prophecy

The next realm of prophecy to understand is that prophecy is a gift (see 1 Corinthians 12:8–10). God gives us this gift so that we can help and encourage people through life's challenges.

Clara was facing chemotherapy after being diagnosed with cancer. She came to church discouraged. At the end of the service she went to the front to receive prayer. The person who prayed for her was unaware of her recent diagnosis. "God has seen your faith. Your faith will be used to help many people during their times of difficulty," the person prophesied. Clara needed that word. It was a word of comfort, edification and strength to her.

For the next six months, Clara went through struggles as a result of her medical treatment. During those times, she would remember how the prophetic word was spoken over her. She meditated on the words. *My faith will be used to help others. God must have a future for me and not death*, she thought. Today, Clara is being used by the Lord to help many people during their hard challenges of life. The gift of prophecy was used to give her the courage to fight through her difficult days.

God may put a "Clara" in front of you. That person may need encouragement. As you operate in the gift of prophecy, you will see the lives of people around you change.

The Spirit of Prophecy

The next realm of prophecy is the spirit of prophecy (see Revelation 19:10). This realm is not a gift but an anointing. The word *anointing* means "unction of the Holy Spirit." It suggests a picture of smearing something with oil. The Holy Spirit releases an empowerment, like oil poured over an individual, so that you can prophesy—even if you are not usually able to prophesy or if prophecy is not your primary gift. The spirit of prophecy activates you to hear the Lord more clearly. You can release a prophetic word with greater confidence during these times.

The Bible records just such an experience (see 1 Samuel 10). Samuel had just anointed Saul with oil and told him that he had been chosen to lead Israel. Saul learned further that he was to go to a certain town, where he would be met by a procession of prophets and join in their prophesying. It happened just as Samuel foretold. Saul met the procession and, to the amazement of those who knew him, the Spirit of God came upon him in power and he began to prophesy.

Though Saul was not a prophet, the prophetic anointing was released on him. The spirit of prophecy enabled him to prophesy along with the prophets. We also see from this story that a person who prophesies may not necessarily be a holy person or even one who is serving God. I discuss the issue of false prophets in my book *Removing the Veil of Deception* (Chosen, 2009).

Even today people can carry a prophetic anointing, but not necessarily operate in the office of prophet. (We will discuss this office in a moment.) Usually the spirit of prophecy is released on an individual or a group of people during worship. Worship sensitizes a person's spirit, causing him to be more aware of the voice of the Lord. In addition, God empowers people who hold the office of prophet to activate others for prophetic ministry. A prophet is gifted to be able to release the spirit of prophecy on others so they can prophesy.

Either of these situations releases people to prophesy with a greater ease and anointing. The presence of God is so strong in these times that anyone willing to use a small amount of faith can prophesy.

I have friends who pastor a church in Canada. Once when I was ministering there, I asked for the ministry team to come to the front in order to pray for anyone who desired prayer. The pastors were mentoring a young man who was hungry to learn about prophecy, and they invited him to join the ministry team.

During the prayer time, the spirit of prophecy was released. Two elements helped to release the spirit of prophecy: We had worshiped the Lord, and I am known for my prophetic gift and was in the meeting. The ministry team had a word of prophecy for each person who came for prayer. Although this young man was fairly new to the things of the Spirit, he received the same anointing as the team and was able to give words of prophecy as well.

It was a memorable evening for him. He fought past his insecurities. He fought past his limited understanding. By the end of the evening, he had taken a new step toward developing his prophetic gift. The spirit of prophecy was used to help him battle through unbelief and reach a new level of maturity in ministry.

The Office of Prophet

The final realm of prophecy is the office of prophet (see Ephesians 2:19–20; 4:11). Even though everyone can prophesy, God does not call everyone to be a prophet. "All are not apostles, are they? All are not prophets, are they? All are not teachers, are they? All are not workers of miracles, are they?" (1 Corinthians 12:29).

Jesus gave the office of prophet to the Church after He rose from the dead and ascended to heaven (see Ephesians 4:11). Prophets are chosen by God's sovereignty and not by man. A person does not become a prophet through any human works he has done. Neither does a person become a prophet by his own goodness. The Bible does not tell us exactly how all prophets are called. We know only that prophets in the Bible had assignments from God that were undeniable; they knew they must obey His call.

Not all prophets function the same way. They all have different personalities and modes of expression. Yet, prophets have a compelling passion to speak for God to His people. Not everyone is willing to acknowledge the gift or accept God's word. Particularly because prophets are often misunderstood, they must fight to develop their gift and remain obedient to the call of God. This realm of prophecy takes time to develop. Often the person called as a prophet goes through years of refining and testing.

Bill Hamon is recognized throughout the world as a modern-day prophet of God. He tells about the development of his gift in his book *Prophets, Pitfalls and Principles.*

> I am able to prophesy over anyone I lay hands on because of this divine gifting to a prophet—God's grace and faith to flow prophetically in this manner. . . . When I was first activated and released in prophetic ministry at the age of 17, I only had faith to prophesy congregational prophecies. After a particular prophetic message was spoken over me the next year, a greater anointing was activated in me. My exposure to personal prophecy increased my faith to prophesy to individuals now and then. . . . Nearly a decade later, however, God sovereignly moved upon me in a meeting one night and enabled me to prophesy personally to all eighty-five people present. At the time I thought that was a once-in-a-lifetime experience, but two weeks later in another meeting I prophesied to one hundred and fifty people. For the next ten years that new understanding of prophetic ministry allowed me the faith and ability to practice it, and in 1979 I began training others to do the same.[1]

Reading this testimony helped me in my fight, for God has called me to this office. My prophetic journey was very similar to Bishop Hamon's. Before reading the book I did not know anyone who had developed the gift that way. I knew some prophets at that time in my life. They were powerful men and women of God but did not prophesy over every person in a meeting. I had been doing that for a couple of years when I discovered Bishop Hamon's book. Before that I battled with my thoughts. *Is it possible to prophesy over every person in a meeting? Are you sure this is God, or could it be your own flesh? Does anyone else minister this way?* Peace and joy flooded my mind and spirit after I won this fight with my thoughts.

We will discuss the office of prophet further in the next chapter.

Are you beginning to see your place in one of these four realms of prophetic gifting? Take a moment to think about this. As you read Scripture, do certain words seem to jump off the page and into your heart? Has the life of someone been touched because you gave a prophetic word of encouragement or counsel? Have you been in a time of worship or ministry when you felt anointed to speak God's word with boldness? Do you know in your "knower" that you have been called to the office of prophet?

Wherever you are in this realm of ministry, you will find that you are growing. And your character as a prophetic person is maturing as well. Let's look now at that aspect of fighting for this gift.

Fight to Align Your Gift with Biblical Character

Every area of Christian growth seems to bring special challenges to grow into Christlikeness. Not one of us is immune to character flaws, and as we fight to mature in prophetic ministry, we may find that these flaws are painfully visible. Yet the prophetic gift will never reach its potential unless we grow in character according to the Bible's standards. Here are three key areas that many people in prophetic ministry encounter.

Fighting to Overcome Wrong Attitudes

The first battle to be fought for character development involves overcoming an attitude that centers on self. This attitude will likely hinder anyone's success in ministry, but those ministering prophetically can find themselves quickly discredited by it. Like a child shouting "Mine!" when reaching for a coveted toy, the focus on self reveals an unhealthy desire for possession.

King Saul was a leader who wanted to "own" the approval of the people. He was not happy when his subjects began to celebrate David's accomplishments.

> The women sang as they played, and said, "Saul has slain his thousands, and David his ten thousands." Then Saul became very angry, for this saying displeased him; and he said, "They have ascribed to David ten thousands, but to me they have ascribed thousands. Now what more can he have but the kingdom?"
>
> *1 Samuel 18:7–8*

Saul was focused on self. He wanted to be the person in the spotlight. He did not want David or anyone else to receive attention. Like a small child, Saul viewed the applause of people as "mine." Due to his character flaws, Saul was never able to develop his leadership gift to its full potential. He failed to fight against the attitude of self.

God is raising up an entire company of prophets and prophetic people today. "Self" must be willing to allow the prophetic gift in others to develop. Prophets need to celebrate the gifting in others rather than trying to own the gift and limit others in their freedom to prophesy.

Fight to Overcome Feelings of Persecution

Another fight for godly character involves dealing with the fear of being persecuted. Let me say this up front: Persecution is part of the job description for prophets and prophetic people. Certain words of correction, direction, ministry confirmation and other words of knowledge are limited to the office of prophet. All believers can speak prophetic words to encourage, comfort and build up. This type of prophecy spoken by believers is not the same level of prophecy that is spoken through those in the office of prophet.

Because of the potential for being misinterpreted and misunderstood, prophets and prophetic people face challenges whenever they speak the words God gives them. If this turns into a phobia, the ministry, which often depends on bold speech, is greatly hampered.

Daniel was a prophet who experienced ongoing persecution while living as a prisoner in Babylon. Because he lived his life dedicated to God in the midst of his captivity, he made some unpopular choices. He refused, for instance, to eat the delicacies from the king's table and lived a lifestyle of fasting (see Daniel 1:8). He refused to turn from worship of God and was thrown into a lions' den. "My God sent His angel and shut the lions' mouths and they have not harmed me, inasmuch as I was found innocent before Him; and also toward you, O king, I have committed no crime" (Daniel 6:22). Speak about persecution! Yet he maintained a godly attitude and was used mightily in ministry.

It seems that time and again those in the office of prophet (and, incidentally, apostles) go through the most difficult challenges in life. Through these battles it is important to understand God's work to develop the character of those to whom He has entrusted this gift. If you are facing this challenge, know that this refining process prepares you to be used by God. When the persecution fight is won, prophets are dead to self and alive to God.

Fight Not to Quit

The next battle to be fought in the area of character development is fighting to keep moving forward and refusing to quit in the face of discouragement. Prophets and prophetic people must overcome the impulse to give up.

If there was ever a person in the Bible who needed to be able to overcome discouragement, I am sure that it was Job. He was a righteous man. He was prosperous and well respected. In one day, however, he lost everything. He lost his children and his home. He lost his material goods and his position in the community. Later, he was stricken with disease. Then instead of comforting Job, his friends added to his pain by criticizing him with religious remarks.

In the midst of his great suffering, Job had to fight against discouragement. He had to fight for his belief in a God who is faithful to us even when the circumstances challenge that perception of goodness. In time, Job was truly overwhelmed with God's mercy, as He revealed His great wisdom and power.

There have been many times when I have had to fight through discouragement. Discouragement is designed to keep us from developing our gifts. It can cause any of us to want to quit.

I will never forget one time when Dale and I were on the verge of quitting our ministry. God had given us a platform that allowed us to minister not only locally, but nationwide. We had poured our lives into people for years. Then a time came when it seemed that everyone we knew turned against us. People spoke lies about us. They made false accusations. People we loved and trusted turned their backs on us. Our minds seemed to be caught in a whirlwind trying to make sense of what was happening.

Dale and I chose to fight when there seemed to be no strength left to fight. Each morning I would wake up and cry out for God's grace to face the day. I remember each morning reminding myself that God was still on His throne, the sun was still shining and the world was still spinning on its axis. Gradually, over a period of weeks, the attacks subsided and the discouragement left. Now I can see that, in the midst of that very difficult time, we grew in ways that we could not have imagined beforehand.

During times of intense battle, we must remember the faithfulness of God. While everyone must fight through times of discouragement for the prophetic gift to be developed, the difficult season is only temporary. If you are going to grow in character, quitting is not an option!

Fighting for Prophetic Sensitivity and Timing

As you find yourself moving in one or more of the realms of prophecy, and as your character is being developed, you will find that you are becoming more adept at prophetic sensitivity and timing.

Timing is an important issue in prophetic ministry. Some people believe that prophetic words must be given at the moment the insight is received. They are fearful that if they do not release the prophetic word immediately they are "quenching the Spirit" (see 1 Thessalonians 5:19). This phrase refers to forbidding the Holy Spirit free access to flow through a person.

I remember attending a home group that allowed the gifts of the Spirit to be released. A woman in that group was learning to prophesy. She felt that she had to release a prophetic word as soon as she sensed the presence of the Lord, but she was terrified at the idea of speaking a prophetic word in front of the home group.

That night, she received a word. We watched, perplexed, as her body tightened, her hands trembled and her eyes grew wide with fear. Suddenly the words burst out: "The Lord loves you! He is here tonight! Let Him cover you with His love!" Then—wham! She fell to the floor exhausted.

Although the word was not harmful—and, as we have learned, it is important not to let the fear of man control our actions—still, there is a right time for prophecy. The woman was out of the right timing for the word to be released. Thus, her word did not edify the people. Had she waited, God could have continued to give her greater revelation in the word so that it benefited the group. Plus, she would have been more assured and peaceful in her delivery.

Developing the prophetic gift can be compared to making good wine. Several years ago, Dale and I visited Napa, California, and drove through the famous vineyards located in that area. As we talked with some of the growers, we became aware of the challenging, lengthy and meticulous process of crushing and refining the grapes in order to bring them to their fullest flavor and potency.

You are similar to God's grapes. Only the winemaker can change grapes into wine. Only the Lord is able to change you from a natural human being into a supernatural prophetic minister. God wants to develop your prophetic gift to be used for His glory. Make yourself available to Him. Fight through every challenge. Watch Him take your yielded life and develop you into the prophetic minister He intended you to be.

Once the Lord develops the prophetic gift in you, there is a possibility that you may be used by God in the office of prophet. Remember, though, not everyone is called to be a prophet. Some are. Some are not. How do you know if you have this calling? And, if so, how do you move from prophesying to becoming a prophet? The next chapter will answer these questions.

Prayer

Lord, I make myself available to You. I want to be used in prophetic ministry. Help me understand the fight involved while developing my prophetic gift. I need Your grace and revelation to be successful in those battles. I refuse any self-serving tendencies. I refuse the feelings of persecution and discouragement. You are my joy in life.

Help me to be aware of Your timing for releasing prophecy. May I be led by Your Spirit and not my emotions. I want my life to bring glory to You. I will continue to allow the development of prophetic ministry to increase in my life. I make a decision today not to stop. I will not quit. I submit myself to Your Spirit. Have Your own way in my life, Holy Spirit. In Jesus' name I pray, Amen.

For Further Reflection

1. Describe the four realms of prophecy. Are you aware of their operation in your life?
2. Has there been a time that you had to fight to release a prophetic word?
3. How do you handle persecution?
4. How do you handle discouragement?
5. What is God's part and what is your part in developing your prophetic gift?

9

FIGHTING TO GROW
IN THE OFFICE OF PROPHET

How did she grow up from a little girl into such a beautiful woman? Every parent of a bride has asked this same question. Images of the little girl struggling as she learned to ride her bike or study for a spelling test come flooding in. Then there are the memories of the challenges she faced when she began dating or selecting a college. Struggles came at each stage of life. Yet, she learned that her future success depended on her faithfulness to the tasks that would prepare her for her destiny. Growth and development, she discovered, is a process. And, today, she stands prepared as a beautiful bride. She is ready for the next challenges in her life that involve being a wife.

Growing from the gift of prophecy to the office of prophet happens the same way. A prophet, once called, is not formed in a day. A prophet must fight to be faithful to the tasks that will prepare him for his calling from God. First, however, must come an anointing for the office.

How to Know If You Are a Prophet

It is God who calls prophets, and not any individual or organization (see 1 Corinthians 12:28; Ephesians 4:11–12). This is a high calling indeed.

Throughout the Bible we find examples of ways that prophets were called by God—some before they were even born. Two examples of men who were anointed as prophets before birth were Jeremiah, in the Old Testament, and the apostle Paul, in the New Testament. God told Jeremiah this: "Before I formed you in the womb I knew you, and before you were born I consecrated you; I have appointed you a prophet to the nations" (Jeremiah 1:5). The apostle Paul wrote that God "set me apart even from my mother's womb and called me through His grace" (Galatians 1:15).

Not every prophet is called before birth or in some unusual way. Bill Hamon is a prophet who began his call merely with an intense hunger to serve the Lord.

> My call to the ministry did not involve a vision, dream, angelic visitation or voice from heaven. Though most people think that in order to be a prophet you must have some unusual, supernatural experience, I received nothing of that nature. All I had received was a growing desire, after I was saved, to become a minister.[1]

Whether you have sensed from an early age that you have a call of God as a prophet or have grown in understanding over the years, you can confirm whether or not you are called to the office of prophet. Here are several ways.

Through a Dream or Vision

God may give you a clear dream or vision that defines your call to the office of prophet. Although many believers experience dreams and visions, a prophet usually experiences them more than others. This manner of communication from God will be a tool that the prophet uses to hear from God throughout his or her time of ministry.

Others Recognize Your Call

Another way to know if you are a prophet is by the recognition of others. When God calls a person as a prophet, others will acknowledge it. People will begin to point out the call of prophet on your life, perhaps in the form of a prophetic word.

Samuel was clearly recognized as a prophet by the people of his day. "All Israel from Dan even to Beersheba knew that Samuel was confirmed as a prophet of the LORD" (1 Samuel 3:20). People throughout the region recognized the call of prophet on his life. They recognized that the Lord's hand was on him to deliver a true word and confirmed the accuracy of his prophetic gift. "Samuel grew and the LORD was with him and let none of his words fail" (1 Samuel 3:19).

The prophet does not need to promote himself; his gift will be revealed. "A man's gift makes room for him and brings him before great men" (Proverbs 18:16).

In some churches and Christian organizations, individuals who are recognized as prophets are invited to be ordained into the office publicly. The word *ordain* refers to recognition that the individual has fulfilled certain preparations and is authorized to perform certain functions for an organization. Ordination does not make a person a prophet; the call of God and proper preparation make a person a prophet. Ordination is simply earth agreeing with heaven.

Knowing in Your Heart

Ultimately, if you are called by God to be a prophet, you will know it in your heart. There will be little doubt. And once you know, you can be assured that you will face difficult days and times of testing.

I once heard the phrase, "Be sure of your call when your back is against the wall." How true that is! If you are a prophet there will be times when you sense you are backed against a wall of resistance. The resistance is there to try to rob you of your call. During those hard times, you must fight the fight of faith and hold on to the call of God. That only happens when a person has the inner assurance that he has been called by God.

Gifts of the Holy Spirit

Another way to know you are called to be a prophet is the frequent and accurate operation of the word of knowledge and the word of wisdom. Those are two of the gifts of the Holy Spirit mentioned in the New Testament (see 1 Corinthians 12:8).

Word of knowledge, as we have noted, refers to the information received by the hearer from the Holy Spirit. The information may be about a person's health, spiritual attitude, conduct or details about the person's life.

Word of wisdom is similar to word of knowledge. The information received through this gift usually involves wise and prudent action that the person needs to take.

A person who has the ability to operate through these gifts to uncover revelation and illumination has the characteristic of a potential prophet.

Heightened Spiritual Discernment

Another way you can tell if you are called to the office of prophet is a propensity for greater spiritual discernment. The gift of discerning of spirits is mentioned in 1 Corinthians 12:10. Prophets generally have a keen sense of the presence of God. Prophets also have keen perception about angelic beings and evil demonic spirits. Often they remember being aware of these unseen spiritual beings throughout their lives. They also usually understand the actions needed to handle these supernatural agents.

Why "Few Are Chosen"

The Bible says that "many are called, but few are chosen" (Matthew 22:14). If so many people are called, in this case as prophet, why are so few chosen? Good question!

I believe it is because the process is so arduous. God does not ask everyone to endure it. Prophets will be judged more strictly than others (see James 3:1) and must be willing to go through the refining process in preparation for their call. The preparation process for a prophet feels like living in a hot furnace. Scripture describes this: "Lo, I have refined thee, and not with silver, I have chosen thee in a furnace of affliction" (Isaiah 48:10, YLT). God uses the adversities and fiery trials of life to test the faith of His prophets. Bill Hamon writes of this place of God's choosing:

> He will plow the prophet upside-down, exposing the root problems, and then He will either spray them with a strong anointing to destroy them or else rake the minister's soul until all the roots are removed and thrown into the fire of God's purging process.[2]

Although Joseph knew about his call, he found himself in Egypt as a slave. He was falsely accused. He spent years in prison. He probably wondered how the dream from so long ago would ever come to pass. "They afflicted his feet with fetters, he himself was laid in irons; until the time that his word came to pass, the word of the LORD tested him" (Psalm 105:18–19). The dream Joseph had concerning his call was tested in difficult circumstances. All of this testing would prepare him for God's high call on his life.

God is serious about choosing His prophets. He wants them to be totally yielded to Him. Selfish ambition and carnal motives, therefore, must be destroyed. This usually takes place in the "furnace of affliction."

It is in that refining place that God purges the person of motives and traits that would be destructive to the gift. God does not destroy the individual, nor does He demand absolute perfection; otherwise a person would never be released from the furnace of affliction. God uses those fiery trials and difficulties to do the work of preparation. "Beloved, do not be surprised at the fiery ordeal among you, which comes upon you for your testing, as though some strange thing were happening to you" (1 Peter 4:12).

As the prophet fights through the difficulties of furnace life, he comes forth like silver or gold. He has new confidence in God's calling. He has a new level of boldness. The prophet is God's servant, prepared to do the will of the Lord.

Boldness without Arrogance

If you are called to this office, you will find that as you make the transition from the gift of prophecy to the office of prophet, your gift will be used in prediction, ministry confirmation, visions, dreams and correction. As you grow, you might have to fight against feelings of failure when your word is judged and not accepted as being from the Lord. You may need to fight for confidence when your leaders adjust your word or bring correction. Remember—correction is not rejection. Fight against any feeling of rejection as you grow in gifting. You are becoming the prophet that God wants you to be.

As you grow in confidence, you will find that there is also a natural tendency to grow in boldness. The mature prophet is often daring, fearless and forceful in his expression of the word he has been given by the Lord. This is not arrogance; it is part of the anointing.

Religious training often causes us to think that we should not be bold in our spirituality. Somehow a quiet and shy person is considered more spiritual. This is not scriptural. God does not desire His people to be timid and bashful in any of the callings and gifts He gives: "God has not given us a spirit of timidity, but of power and love and discipline" (2 Timothy 1:7). It is important to realize that this is one way the enemy subdues prophets into relinquishing their call. The enemy wants to stop them from advancing in ministry.

I spent years fighting timidity. I thought it was my personality. I did not understand that timidity is not a gift from God; it is an assignment from the enemy. Inside me was a bold person whom God wanted to use. "We have confidence to enter the holy place by the blood of Jesus" (Hebrews 10:19).

Once I realized that God wanted me to function in boldness, I entered the battle to force myself to move out of timidity. I determined to open my mouth and speak boldly. The more I fought against timidity and embraced boldness, the stronger I became. Today, it is hard for me to think I was ever timid and shy. The Lord strengthened me in my battle. I am now the bold person He created me to be. If you struggle with timidity, let me assure you that He will do the same thing in your life.

Boldness, remember, is not arrogance. Although the Lord wants His prophets to be bold, a haughty and prideful spirit has no place in the life of the prophet.

Solomon is an example of a man whose boldness became misguided. Called and chosen by God, he started his ministry with a good heart. Solomon was a man of prayer, and God entrusted him with great wealth and wisdom. Later in life, however, due to pride, greed and self-confidence, Solomon had his kingdom taken away from him (see 1 Kings 11). In the book of Ecclesiastes, he wrote of his misery toward the end of his life. He had failed to allow his heart to be purified and to forsake sin. Solomon's tragic end could have been prevented if he had been willing to allow God's refining process to be revealed in the furnace of affliction.

Solomon's wealth, fame and honor came during a time when he was yielded to the purpose of God. When he began to think that he had made himself great, Solomon was on a slippery downhill path. He was deceived to think that his human abilities had elevated him.

Those called to be prophets must fight to remain humble while simultaneously being bold for the Lord.

Merchandising the Gift

Having a humble spirit can help protect the prophet from getting off-track. Believe it or not, when a prophet gains a reputation for releasing true words from God, the temptation will arise to sell the gift for money. I refer to this as "merchandising the gift."

Occasionally we hear reports of ministers who promise a prophetic word for a large sum of money. Others will also use a prophetic word to control or manipulate a person. The person may be promised the blessings of God if he serves that minister. True prophets must be free from the love of money. They must also deal with any character flaws of selfish ambition or the desire to control the lives of those they minister to.

This temptation is as old as the Bible.

The story of Balaam reveals how this temptation works. (See Numbers 22–24.) The people of Israel were victorious in battle after battle as they headed from Egypt toward their Promised Land. Balak, king of Moab, was terrified by the large number of Israelites camping through the plains, and wanted to drive them out of his country. To help achieve this plan, Balak decided to call Balaam to come and curse them.

Balaam may have been a true prophet of God at some point, since he had a reputation for giving accurate prophetic words. Thus, Balak sent elders and princes to the prophet Balaam with this proposal: If he would come and curse Israel, Balak would pay him the appropriate fee. Balaam sought the Lord's counsel, and told the messengers to go back home, for the Lord would not let him go.

Balak responded by sending a more distinguished entourage with the promise of a handsome reward if he would come and curse the Israelites. He was being tested to see if he would be faithful to God or merchandise the gift. This time he accepted their offer. Balaam appeared at three places designated by Balak, but each time Balaam spoke, the Lord told him to bless Israel and not to curse it.

It is sad to see that in the end the temptation was apparently too much for Balaam. He appears to have started faithfully, but he allowed pride and selfish ambition to enter his heart. "Forsaking the right way, they have gone astray, having followed the way of Balaam, the son of Beor, who loved the wages of unrighteousness" (2 Peter 2:15). Balaam apparently merchandised the gift of God. He failed to fight against the love of money. We will talk more about money in relation to prophecy in the next chapter.

Fear of the Lord or Fear of Man

Throughout the life of the prophet, he or she will be challenged with choices. These choices will determine the success or failure of the gift. One of the most critical choices a prophet will make involves choosing the right kind of fear.

In chapter 7, I mentioned my fight to overcome the fear of man. I had to replace the fear of man with the fear of the Lord. The fear of the Lord is not a cringing, tormenting fear. It is a holy awe of God. The fear of the Lord has to do with a deep love for God and His purposes. It means that we want to please the Lord and bring honor and glory to His name. We must, therefore, be constantly aware of our motives when releasing the prophetic gift.

Prophets are called by God to root out things in people and situations that are not from God. They are used by God to clean up the lives of individuals, churches or territories. "I have appointed you this day over the nations and over the kingdoms, to pluck up and to break down, to destroy and to overthrow, to build and to plant" (Jeremiah 1:10).

Jeremiah was a prophet. The words God had for him to deliver were not always pleasant. They were words of correction. They were words that exposed sin and unrighteousness. Hard words like this, as I mentioned earlier, are reserved for the office of prophet.

Persons growing in the prophetic gifting might sometimes receive hard words. If you find the Lord is leading you in this way, my counsel is to share the word with a mature leader. Allow the leader to determine if you should deliver the word or merely pray about it. Sometimes hard words are just a call to intercession for the person or circumstance. The leader might, however, sense that the word is accurate and that it is time to deliver the word. If so, ask the leader or someone he or she trusts to be with you when you speak the word. This will help you grow in your gift and feel confident that the word has been judged for accuracy. If this happens to you on a consistent basis, God may be preparing you to grow into the office of a prophet.

The fear of man and man's opinion will attempt to stop the prophet in his assignment from God. He must fight to be obedient to the will of the Lord. God's word to the prophet might not be a word that he wants to deliver. It may uncover sin, require repentance or some other unpopular response from the hearer. The prophet must fight, therefore, to be submitted to God's will and free from the fear of man.

The Question of Spiritual Accountability

One of the ways to keep your ministry pure from pride, arrogance, greed, the fear of man and many other temptations is through spiritual accountability. For several years there has been a great deal of controversy concerning the often-used term *spiritual covering*. I sat on a panel of prophetic leaders recently to discuss the scriptural validity of this term. Several participants explained why they did not endorse its use:

- *Jesus is my covering.*
- *I am covered in the blood of Jesus.*
- *I cannot find a Scripture saying that I need to be "covered."*

The discussion was lively! At the end of the day, all of us seemed comfortable with the term *spiritual accountability*.

Whether we refer to "covering" or "accountability," we all need someone to speak truth into our lives. Prophets are not exempt! We all have blind spots. There are issues in our lives that we are unaware of. The more influence we have and the stronger the prophetic gift becomes in our lives, the greater danger we are to the Body of Christ.

In the Old Testament, the anointed priest was required to bring a greater sin offering than the average individual (see Leviticus

4:3, 27–28). I believe this was because the anointed priest was in a position to affect more people by his sin. The New Testament reveals the same principle for leaders. "Let not many of you become teachers, my brethren, knowing that as such we will incur a stricter judgment" (James 3:1). Everyone needs someone to be accountable to. These individuals will help us fight to keep the prophetic ministry pure before the Lord.

In the Old Testament we find that the Tabernacle and its furniture had coverings (see Exodus 26:7, 14; Numbers 4:11–12). The priests who ministered for the Lord had special garments or coverings (see Exodus 28:42). We also find that God's people are covered with a robe of righteousness (see Isaiah 61:10). These pictures help us understand God's desire for spiritual covering or accountability in the lives of His prophets (see Ephesians 5:21).

Chuck Pierce addresses the issue of spiritual covering in his book *The Best Is Yet Ahead.*

> Covering means protection, concealing, warmth, hidden from view, or being in a place of safety. Being in proper alignment with authority produces these things in our lives. If we have not moved out from under our place of authority, the enemy has far fewer means of attacking us because we are covered or hidden from his view.[3]

I lead a network of pastors, ministry leaders and marketplace leaders. They look to me for spiritual accountability in their lives. I also have spiritual accountability for my own life. No person reaches a place of perfection. We need people who will help us reach our destiny. These people help us discover areas of character and gifting that need to be adjusted.

Frequently we read about leaders who are involved in immoral lifestyles, embezzling money from the ministry or other evils. Many times these leaders are not protected by spiritual accountability. They need bold leaders who will confront their wrong behavior for the purpose of restoration.

These accountability leaders should not operate out of control or domination. A heart of mercy and words of truth are necessary for restoration in the prophet's life. "Lovingkindness and truth have met together; righteousness and peace have kissed each other" (Psalm 85:10). Counsel that gives mercy void of truth will cause the prophet to stray from God's path. Direction that gives truth without mercy will end in legalism and hardness of heart. Accountability leaders should be full of God's mercy and His truth. Spiritual accountability helps the prophet fight a good fight against every trap that the enemy sends to hinder or stop his gift.

Consider, for example, the use of the revelation gifts of the Holy Spirit. These revelation gifts are word of wisdom, word of knowledge and discerning of spirits, and they are given to a prophet to assure accuracy in the words he or she gives (see 1 Corinthians 12). As you begin to operate in these gifts in relation to the office of prophet, it is helpful to have someone more spiritually mature judge each revelation. A pastor, elder or other spiritual leader can listen to the word you believe God is speaking to you and confirm its accuracy.

The process of accountability will keep you safe from releasing words that may not come from the Lord. The process will also give you confidence in your gift.

Keeping Prophecy on Course

A few years ago, I joined leaders in another roundtable discussion—this time about the need for accountability by those who are in the office of prophet. Although all believers need accountability, this is especially necessary for those who are in the office of prophet. Prophets are not perfect and should always operate in a spirit of humility and a willingness to have their words and character judged. The discussion group, part of which was devoted to the topic of unfulfilled or wrong prophecies, included about fifteen prophetic ministers who were also authors—people mature and seasoned in prophetic ministry.

The gathering came about in response to a new book on the topic of modern-day prophecy. The author had documented numerous examples of people who had been wounded due to either unfulfilled prophecies or prophecies that resulted in casualties in their lives.

Around that table we wondered: How could this happen? Is there a way to embrace modern-day prophecy without people experiencing hurts and wounds and rejecting the entire prophetic movement? How should we handle prophecies or prophets that are false? What are some safeguards for receiving or releasing prophecy? How do we fight to see the fulfillment of our own prophetic promises?

At the end of the evening we still did not have all the answers we wanted. Each of us did, however, make a commitment to work toward taking the prophetic movement to a new level of excellence. We agreed that we cannot reject what God is doing merely because some people are not using wisdom in receiving or releasing prophetic ministry. We must find a better way for the operation of true prophetic ministry in today's world. That meeting made me more determined than ever to be part of the solution and, I hope, not part of the problem! Much of the solution, I realized, includes educating, equipping, activating and releasing people to fulfill their God-given calling.

If you are called to be a prophet, know that you have an awesome responsibility. Take your gift seriously! God has made a way for you to represent Him in the earth realm. He has planned for you to deliver His word and plans to the inhabitants of the earth. Your prophetic spirit requires intense training, humility and submission to the Lord and to other ministries. God's rigid discipline in your life keeps you safe and keeps the Body of Christ safe from deception, abuses, wounding in the Body and many other evils.

You cannot afford to take any shortcuts into ministry. The cost for the prophet personally and for God's people is too high. I always ask the Lord to remind me of Paul's words when he was speaking to the Corinthians: "But I discipline my body and make it my slave, so that, after I have preached to others, I myself will not be disqualified" (1 Corinthians 9:27). Stay qualified as God's prophet!

Like all believers who operate in prophetic ministry, God's true prophets are not confined to church buildings. Whether you are a believer who is given an occasional prophetic word or a prophet called from the womb, your gifting is not limited to operation in the congregational setting: You are called to share this ministry in the marketplace. The next chapter will help you understand how your prophetic ministry operates in that arena.

Prayer

Thank You, Lord, for raising up true prophets today. Whether or not I am called to this office, I ask You to help me be faithful to the process of growing in ministry. I resist all timidity that hinders me from releasing Your word in boldness. I reject all pride and arrogance that comes to pollute my gift. I reject the fear of man. I reject the love of money and refuse to merchandise the gift You have given me.

Lord, I ask You to align me with the right spiritual covering. I will make myself accountable for my life and for my gift. I come to You in a spirit of humility and ask You to fill me with the fear of the Lord. My desire is to please You in all that I do. Help all those who are called to this office to stay on the path that leads from the gift of prophecy to prophet. Let each life bring honor and glory to You. In Jesus' name I pray, Amen.

For Further Reflection

1. What are some of the ways God uses to call prophets?
2. How does a person know he or she is a prophet?
3. Describe the furnace of affliction. What happens in this place?
4. How does a prophet merchandise the gift of God?
5. Why does a prophet need the fear of the Lord in his or her life?
6. If you believe God has called you to this office, what is your next step?

10

FIGHTING TO RELEASE PROPHECY IN THE MARKETPLACE

"You will prophesy to rulers and leaders in many nations."

How would I ever do that? I wondered. At that time in my life, when I was given this word of prophecy, I did not know, for starters, how I could possibly even get to different nations. In those days the average person did not consider flying to distant lands. Businesspeople might make such a trip, and certain missionaries, and someone taking an exotic vacation. And what about prophesying to rulers and leaders? I was learning to prophesy over a few individuals, but certainly not on a national scale.

Prophecy as I knew it was usually released inside a church building. I had never heard of prophesying to government and business leaders outside church walls. Yet, today, I find myself fulfilling what was prophesied over me so many years ago.

The world is desperate to hear the word of God—and God is using people who are speaking out with prophetic boldness to get His message out. It starts with the right "mentality."

Fighting between a Greek and a Hebrew Mindset

Anyone who desires to be used in prophetic ministry in the marketplace must have a biblical Hebrew mindset as opposed to a "Greek" mentality. By this I mean that we need a biblical worldview if we are going to accomplish God's purposes in the earth.

Greek Influence

The Church has traditionally been indoctrinated with a certain aspect of ancient Greek thinking. This mindset is "dualistic," the conflicting relationship between two independent elements such as matter and spirit. Rather than biblical precepts, philosophers such as Plato, Aristotle and Plotinus have molded the thinking of many believers. Plato was very instrumental in the way we think. He believed that the world was divided into two levels. He believed that the upper level consisted of eternal ideas and the lower level was temporal and physical. The highest level was considered superior to the temporary and imperfect world of matter. Work and occupations were part of the lower level.

Religious people who embraced Plato's philosophy and its derivatives came to believe that the marketplace, with its physical labors and occupations, was "carnal." They believed that the marketplace dealt with earthly things such as business and money. Spiritual Christians did not need to be involved in these earthly and worldly areas. This mindset also holds that humankind is supreme. This philosophy is called secular humanism. During the time that Greek philosophers rose to prominence, the upper-level "spiritual" people were considered far superior to the temporary and imperfect world of matter. Lower-level people, like market-place people, were considered inferior and unspiritual.

Biblical Hebrew Thinking

The Bible paints a different picture for us. A biblical mindset takes the position that God is supreme in the universe, not humans. Truth does not come from human reason but from divine reve-lation. The ancient Hebrew people, who broke from pagan society to follow the one true God, were able to recognize His presence and His word in, through and over all of creation. They believed that God was involved in every aspect of their lives, including their work. As a result, they believed that work is a form of ministry.

God is shifting the thinking of many Christians today from a "Greek mindset" to a "Hebrew mindset." We are realizing that our work is a holy calling from God. Os Hillman, in his book *Faith & Work: Do They Mix?,* addresses this concept. Below is his response to a letter he received after writing a devotional for men and women in the marketplace.

> One day I received a very simple note from a pastor that said, "How can a businessman have such great wisdom?" This comment spoke volumes to me. Basically, he was im-plying that clergy were the only ones in tune with the spiri-tual matters of life, and businessmen and women focused on the "secular" life. However, God never said this. He is now helping many of us begin to understand our true calling as disciples of the Lord Jesus, but with different roles to fulfill in the body of Christ. And no role is less holy than another.[1]

Prophetic Strategies for Success

God is bringing fresh revelation to the Church concerning min-istry in the marketplace. Here are several strategies for success in reaching out with prophetic ministry.

Embracing a Holy Call

Understanding that the call to bring God's revelation to the marketplace is a high and holy call is the first prophetic strategy for success. "We are his workmanship, created in Christ Jesus for good works, which God prepared beforehand so that we would walk in them" (Ephesians 2:10). Knowing that God calls you to the marketplace can help you fulfill your purpose as a prophetic person.

Michael was a successful businessman. He had received several awards for both his inventions and his quality of work. After he received the baptism with the Holy Spirit, Michael sensed a new passion for the Lord. He loved his times of worship and reading the Bible. People started recognizing the skills he had in dealing with people. "You are called to be a pastor," they told him.

"Really?" he said. "A pastor?" Perhaps that explained the new zeal for God that he was experiencing.

Ready to believe that this was God's direction for his life, Michael quit his job and accepted the position as pastor of a young church. The next couple of years were misery for Michael. Being a pastor was not what he expected. Dealing with people's problems, preaching several times a week and overseeing financial difficulties soon turned his zeal into drudgery. He resigned and went back to the business he loved. Day after day he found that God was using him right where he was.

After returning to the marketplace, his zeal for God returned. The spiritual gifts that he thought were reserved for use in church buildings were used in every part of his life. Michael was now free to be the prophetic man God had created him to be.

Releasing Prophetic Gifts and Faith

The second prophetic strategy is to bring both your gifts and faith into the marketplace. God's prophetic promises are available for believers in everyday work situations. It starts by learning to listen for His voice.

My husband worked for most of his life as an engineer, usually in manufacturing plants. When problems surfaced at work, Dale knew that God had the solutions he needed. Occasionally, for instance, some piece of equipment would break. Experts would be brought in to identify the problems. Often, after much testing, the experts could not find the problem. Dale's response was to pray. He would hear the voice of the Lord with the solution for whatever problems came up.

Every time Dale identified the true cause of the equipment failure, the workers would always ask the same question. "How did you know that?" Since the experts did not have the answers, they wanted to know how Dale had the answers.

He would always reply, "I prayed."

After this occurred a number of times, the workers would start to ask the question, then they would stop and say, "I know. You prayed." They seemed perplexed that God could give direction about broken equipment. As they continued to see the success-ful solutions that came as a result of prayer, however, they were convinced. God is a speaking God. He wants to communicate with His people in every situation. He has the answers to all of the difficulties of life.

Over a period of time the coworkers realized that Dale had brought his faith and prophetic gifts into the workplace. He was successful in his work because he worked with God.

Taking Care in Your Delivery

Another prophetic strategy for success in the workplace is adapting the words to the situation. If prophetic words are de-livered in a way that does not sound religious, and if the words are easily understood by the hearer, they can be a powerful tool to draw unbelievers to the reality of the true God.

There have been times when I have spoken prophetic words over governmental, educational and business leaders in anti-Christian nations. I am careful to follow the Lord's leading in these situations. When I speak about a biblical character, for instance, I might not say the name of the person; a Jewish name might cause someone in an anti-Christian culture to reject what I am saying. When I use a verse from the Bible to prophesy, I call it "a saying."

By receiving wisdom from the Lord about strategies like these, I have been able to gain the favor of God from various international leaders. I find that they give me permission to fulfill God's purposes in those anti-Christian places. We have been granted permission for some of the humanitarian projects we wanted to do, for instance. The words of knowledge and prophecy touch the hearts of these leaders. After that, they do not mind that I am a woman and a Christian. The hearts of these unbelieving leaders are touched by the one true God through a prophetic word.

On one such occasion, our team was attempting to establish humanitarian help in a war-torn nation. I asked a government leader if I could give him a "word of encouragement." Everyone in that ravaged land needed encouragement. He readily agreed. In a word of prophecy I described events that he had experienced as a child and also as a leader in his nation. I continued by letting him know that the God that I serve wanted to encourage him in his efforts for his nation. The man knew that I was a Christian.

Following the "word of encouragement" the man looked at me. "You can do anything in this nation that you want to do. You can come to my office every day. If anyone causes you problems, tell him to come to me." The unbelieving man realized that the God I serve, the True and Living God, is real. The prophetic word, carefully spoken, opened the nation to our team so we could help the innocent people who were victims of devastation.

Overcoming Hindrances

The next prophetic strategy for success is learning to overcome hindrances by delivering the prophetic word with the wisdom of God. You may not be called to prophesy over world leaders, but you might be called to prophesy over the people you work with. You will need to fight against any mindset that tries to reserve prophecy for church gatherings. A religious spirit will tend to limit the release of God's gifting.

There are several considerations to remember when you face difficulties prophesying in the marketplace. Following are only a few that I want to mention. These principles have helped me fight against ungodly hindrances that are designed to stop God's purposes from being released.

- Ask the Lord to give you the wisdom you need to deliver the word. Ask for the right timing. The person needs to be ready to receive it.

- Ask the person for permission to speak what you sense "on the inside" for him or her. It is important not to pour out prophecy just because you sense it. Always get permission to do this. So far, I have never had one person turn me down. I usually say that I sense a "word of encouragement" for the person. Everyone wants to be encouraged!

- Fight against any feelings of being in a "secular" place. A religious spirit will try to keep you from being obedient to the Lord. God has sent you to the marketplace as His prophetic person to do His work and to speak His mind and wisdom.

Offering Prophetic Intercession

Another strategy for success in the marketplace includes prophetic intercession.

Intercessors—meaning, simply, people who are willing to pray—can hear the heart of God and bring before Him whatever He wants them to pray. We call this "prophetic intercession." I wrote about this type of praying in my book *Prophetic Intercession*.

> We are not praying for ourselves, but for others. Putting the two words together, "prophetic intercession" means:

- Seeking God's presence in order to converse
- Meeting with God and hearing Him on behalf of others
- As a result of seeking, meeting with and hearing God
- Then, speaking forth the mind and counsel of God

> In prophetic intercession, we come into the presence of the Lord and hear His mind and counsel. We are then able to pray the things that are on His heart. Too often we pray the things that are on our heart and fail to hear Him. It is through seeking, hearing and speaking forth His mind that we see powerful breakthroughs occur.[2]

Prophetic intercessors are vital in helping bring success to those in the marketplace. They can pray the mind and counsel of God for the places of work. What has God promised for this business? What does He want to happen in this place? They are willing to fight for God's purposes and His righteousness to be released. They pray for integrity, and they fight in prayer against corrupt practices.

On a recent ministry trip I was asked to pray over the office of a Christian dentist. He had had a successful practice in his town for more than thirty years. During the previous three months, however, the practice had come to a standstill. Suddenly, no one called or made appointments. There was no explanation for the change.

When we arrived at the office, the dentist tried to open the front door. He could not get the door open, and we had to enter through a back door. There was no reason for the front door to be stuck. This had never happened before. I had a prophetic revelation that we were dealing with an assignment of the enemy to keep the door to the clinic closed to patients in order to dry up his finances. The closed front door was a prophetic picture of what was happening in the spirit realm.

After anointing the front door with oil, I led us in prophetic intercession. "Father, I thank You that this business belongs to You. This is a business that is established for Kingdom purposes. This owner walks in covenant with You. I command every evil force that is attempting to keep the door closed to be stopped. I say to the door of this clinic, 'Open and allow the patients to come in.' I command the phones to ring with people calling who need the help of this dentist. We thank You, Lord, for an increase in this business. In Jesus' name we pray."

I knew that a spiritual opening had occurred. The closed door could no longer keep patients away from the clinic.

A few days later, the dentist was excited to report on what had occurred. "It happened the way you prayed," he said with enthusiasm. He told how the phones started ringing the next morning after we prayed. In fact, it was hard for those answering the phones to keep up with all the appointments people were scheduling. The evil assignment to close the door on that business was broken.

Various ministries are actually training intercessors to pray for businesses. After attending several of these training sessions, a friend of mine named Glenda realized the importance of praying for the place where she works. She hoped that perhaps four or five people at work would be willing to pray with her.

The next day Glenda asked her boss for permission to invite other workers to pray with her for the business to be successful. She had planned to ask them to gather before work. After hearing her request, her boss said he did not want them praying before work: He wanted them to pray during working hours! He recognized that the business needed divine intervention.

To Glenda's astonishment, 65 people came to pray. She had no idea that that many people at her workplace were interested in God or prayer. As they joined together, a new sense of peace came into the building. Businessmen in suits stood with tears streaming down their faces as they prayed. Coworkers talked in a congenial manner to one another. People recognized that something supernatural was happening as a result of prayer at their place of work. What a change!

Later, many changes were made in the business. Corrupt and immoral businesspeople were exposed and fired. New leaders were brought in. Employees were told that the business would be operated with integrity. Prayer for the marketplace works!

Employing Paid Intercessors

Some businesses are hiring prophetic intercessors to pray for their companies. This concept of payment for prayer is new to a lot of people. We pay pastors. We often pay worship leaders. Yet, the thought of paying intercessors is foreign to many church people. Others recognize that some of these intercessors spend many hours each day in prayer. It makes sense to them to compensate these intercessors for the time they spend praying for their businesses.

Certain guidelines must be followed to provide legal protection for the businesses. One of those guidelines is that no one should be forced to participate in corporate prayer meetings. They also do not reject anyone from joining in prayer or cause anyone to feel like an outcast due to his or her religious beliefs.

Prophetic intercessors should pray for *all* of the workers to perform in excellence. A spirit of excellence causes everyone in the business to benefit. They pray for God to bless people of all faiths, and pray for the blessings of God to be on the employees and the business.

Prophetic intercessors are in a battle. They are not just fighting to release God's prophetic promises to the workplace; they are also in a battle against unpopular opinions concerning their calling. They are in a battle against discouraging financial reports. They battle against ungodly immorality in the workplace.

My friend Tommi Femrite heads a network of paid prophetic intercessors. She has written reports providing tangible proof that intercession has benefitted the companies that hired the intercessors. Her intercessors fight for God's prophetic promises to be released in the workplace they pray for. They know that they are part of the strategies for success in the marketplace.

Money and Mammon

In the area of prophetic ministry in the marketplace, one area of concern that arises is the appropriate attitude toward money. Businesspeople who agree to the idea of prayer often have financial needs. Yet Christians are sometimes cautious about praying for money. Isn't it wrong for a Christian to ask God for riches?

There is a misconception here. The word they are thinking of is *mammon*, which deals with worldly riches. The New Testament refers to it as a false god that fills the heart of its worshipers with greed, covetousness and materialism. "No man can serve two masters: for either he will hate the one, and love the other; or else he will hold to the one, and despise the other. [You] cannot serve God and mammon" (Matthew 6:24, KJV). Mammon is often used to describe the gain of earthly riches through ungodly means. It is one of the areas that prophetic intercessors usually target for prayer in the marketplace.

Many Christians who believe that money is mammon also tend to believe that money is the root of evil. The Bible does not teach that. Rather, it says: "The love of money is a root of all sorts of evil, and some by longing for it have wandered away from the faith and pierced themselves with many griefs" (1 Timothy 6:10).

Money is not the problem. The "love of money" is the bad root for all evil. Businesspeople need money to run their businesses. Kingdom-minded businesses create finances for God's purposes. Intercessors help them fight against the god of mammon. They can love God and make money at the same time.

Many times I have asked business owners and marketplace workers to forgive church clergy for what we have taught them. Many clergymen and women have made people in the marketplace feel like second-class citizens in the Kingdom of God. I ask them to forgive us for making them feel as though they love mammon because they want to make money. When I do this, men and women stand with tears streaming down their faces. They have fought with this confusing mindset for years. They love God. They love their work. They want to make money. They want their money to be used for God's purposes in the earth. Some of those purposes may be building orphanages, feeding the poor or other humanitarian projects. They do not want to love money or mammon. Bringing understanding of the fight for God's prophetic promises for the marketplace helps set them free.

Anointing in the Marketplace

A marketplace person was the first person in the Bible who, we are told, was full of the Spirit and anointed by God. Bezalel was a craftsman whose skill was used in the tent of meeting, the Ark of the testimony, the mercy seat upon it and all the furniture of the tent. "See, I have called by name Bezalel, the son of Uri, the son of Hur, of the tribe of Judah. I have filled him with the Spirit of God in wisdom, in understanding, in knowledge, and in all kinds of craftsmanship" (Exodus 31:2–3).

God fills His marketplace people with His Sprit. He has a prophetic purpose for this: He uses them to bring an abundance of blessings and increase to every region and every nation on earth.

We have noted how God raised up a prophetic leader by the name of Joseph who had a worldwide ministry. When God gave him a dream about his future, Joseph saw that he would be in a place of leadership. After sharing his dream with his brothers, the fight for his prophetic destiny really began!

Joseph went through many years of persecution, false accusations, prison and other difficult challenges in life. Through it all, Joseph continued his inward fight to reach his prophetic destiny in the marketplace. He was destined for increase and blessings from God.

Os Hillman writes about the meaning of Joseph's name.

> The meaning of the name Joseph is "God will increase," "May He Add" and "Increase." When the Bible speaks of Joseph, it says that God was aware of his plight and that God was blessing Joseph. "The Lord was with Joseph and he prospered, and he lived in the house of his Egyptian Master" (Genesis 39:20). Even though he was a slave, God described him as being prospered by God.[3]

Eventually, the fight was worth it. Joseph was elevated to second-in-command in Egypt. God put an anointing on his life, giving him strategy for the future. Joseph knew that a time of famine would come to the land, so he could prepare a nation for the difficult days ahead. Through his prophetic gift, Joseph brought increase and blessings to many nations.

This Anointing Is Available Today

Today, there is a "Joseph Anointing" for people in the marketplace. The anointing is the presence and person of the Lord Jesus (see Acts 10:38). God's plan is for His Josephs of today to bring an increase of blessing to the people of the earth, so that the finances can be used for Kingdom purposes.

These prophetic marketplace men and women must war against humanistic philosophy. They must battle against religious thinking that limits God's prophetic gifts to operation only in church buildings. They must battle skepticism to find openings to speak God's prophetic word in the marketplace. They must fight against any love for mammon. They must grow in the understanding of prophetic intercession in order to cause breakthroughs in the workplace.

Many of these people are being used to release prophetic promises over territories and nations. The next chapter will help us see how the release of prophetic promises is used on this grand scale. What an exciting time we live in! Get ready to have your prophetic vision enlarged for God's earth.

Prayer

Thank You, Lord, for raising up prophets and prophetic people in the marketplace. May Your word and Your promises be released in my workplace. I ask You to use my place of work for Kingdom purposes. I decree that corruption, immorality and greed be cleansed from my workplace. I renounce the god of mammon. I love God and desire financial blessings for His purposes.

Lord, I ask You to put a "Joseph Anointing" on my life. Open doors for me to pray and to prophesy Your word and will into the marketplace. I will intercede for success in the workplace. I desire to be blessed so that I can be a blessing in Your Kingdom. Thank You for increase as I fight for the prophetic promises in my workplace. In Jesus' name I pray, Amen.

For Further Reflection

1. What is humanism? Why is it opposed to the purposes of God?
2. Describe a biblical Hebrew mindset.
3. What are some points of wisdom when prophesying in the marketplace?
4. What does the god of mammon do?
5. How do you think a "Joseph Anointing" would help you in the marketplace?

11

FIGHTING FOR PROPHETIC FULFILLMENT IN TERRITORIES AND NATIONS

"What should I do?" the pastor asked. I listened over the phone as the pastor from a developing nation told me his story. An intercessor from his country had spoken a prophetic word that had received national attention. The word revealed that judgment was coming on their country in the form of disasters, which were due to bring major destruction by a certain date.

Fear gripped many in his country after the prophetic word became public. They had already experienced destruction and many deaths due to a fairly recent national disaster.

After listening to the story I began to ask questions.

- Who gave the prophecy?
- Who judged the word?
- How was the prophecy released to the nation?

The answers to these questions helped me to know how to respond. The pastor told how a woman who serves as an intercessor gave the prophetic word, which was recorded during a service. She is not a prophet. In fact, she attends a church that does not believe true prophets exist today. The pastor told me that no one with anointing in the office of prophet had judged the word before it was released to the public.

The woman's pastor, who most likely had not been trained to judge prophecy since his church does not endorse modern-day prophets, pronounced that the word was accurate and gave permission for it to be released. Since the church is large and influential, and since copies of the prophecy were passed around outside of that congregation, the word spread quickly throughout the Christian community in the nation.

The pastor who called me needed counsel on how to handle the growing fear in his nation. My first advice to him was that he should stay within his own area of influence. He should work with his own congregation and the churches that look to him for oversight. He could teach them how to judge prophecy, and also teach them the principles for releasing a prophetic word over a territory or a nation. Once his people were trained in prophetic ministry, they would know what to do with words that do not line up with correct prophetic protocol.

A year later, the pastor told me how he handled the situation. After judging the word, his congregation and the pastors felt that it was not from the Lord. His church and those aligned with him were able to dismiss the prophecy. They received peace in the situation. When the prophesied date passed without a national disaster in their country, the people whom the pastor had trained admired his courage and wisdom. They expressed gratitude to have someone who understands the proper way to respond when questionable prophetic words are released.

We are in a spiritual battle to have God's true word released in territories and nations rather than false words that create fear and confusion.

Protocol Regarding Prophetic Words for Nations

Through the years I have heard many prophecies over various nations. I usually ask these same questions when I hear these words. The first question is, "Who gave the prophecy?"

If it was an individual who is not in the office of prophet, for example an intercessor or someone who prophesies only occasionally, I go to the next question.

The next question is, "Who were the prophets who judged the word?"

Anyone who receives a word and who is not a prophet should submit the word for verification. This is very important when the prophetic word involves judgment on or disaster for a nation. By observing this protocol, the ones who give the word as well as the ones who will hear it have a safeguard in place.

Prophets who are recognized as accurate and credible should judge the word. These prophets should have a proven track record. That means they are known for releasing prophetic words that have proven to be from the Lord.

A prophecy that speaks of judgment, direction or national consequences should be judged by several prophets who have wide spheres of influence. "Let two or three prophets speak, and let the others pass judgment" (1 Corinthians 14:29). These seasoned prophets need to be in agreement with the prophetic word before it is released to a nation.

Samuel in the Old Testament was such a prophet. "Samuel grew and the LORD was with him and let none of his words fail" (1 Samuel 3:19). The Lord caused the words of Samuel to manifest. He was a prophet with a proven record of accuracy; therefore, the people could trust the words that he delivered. His words did not fail, because they came from the Lord.

The third question to ask is, "How is the word to be released?" Usually there are various ways to get a credible prophetic word released within a nation. Churches, gatherings of pastors and leaders, intercession groups, the Internet and various forms of media can be used for releasing a prophetic word. The important thing is to make the word available to those who will know how to respond.

Sometimes intercession will be needed regarding these words. There might be a need to pray for repentance and God's mercy on a nation. Worship gatherings may be called for. At other times, God may want to prepare people by warning them about the future.

I was part of a certain group of prophets for several years. We met on a regular basis for the purpose of hearing what the Lord wanted to say to our nation. When a prophet had a prophetic word, the others in the group would judge it. If we felt the word needed to be released to the public, the word was written down. All the prophets read the word and signed a statement that they were in agreement with it. After that, various ways were used to release it.

Obviously not every prophet in our nation was part of that group. Other groups use different protocols for judging prophecy. Whatever method is used, it is important that some type of protocol be in place. Otherwise, situations similar to the one I mentioned earlier can happen. Wrong prophecies are released. Fear grips the people. Nothing happens, and the world decides that the Church is a bunch of crazies. This should not be!

Note also that not all prophetic words should be made public. Often, when intercessors and leaders meet to pray, they will prophesy over their territories. These words might be direction for that prayer time only and are not meant for public dispersing.

Prophetic Release Brings Breakthrough

God is releasing prophetic voices today that are shattering the plans of the enemy. His voice through these servants is piercing the spiritual darkness over territories and nations. God's prophetic word destroys the evil strongholds of the enemy and causes the plans of the Lord to succeed.

I told the story in my book *Prophetic Intercession* of a prayer meeting of leaders in September 1989 in Europe. During the meeting, powerful intercessors stood and spoke prophetically over various nations that were under oppressive governments. They commanded the walls to fall and the people to be set free.

One man who prayed in that historic prayer meeting prayed this way: "Lord, I come to You like Moses. I bring every prayer that has ever been prayed since the inception. I stand spiritually before the wall of Hungary and I say, 'Let my people go!' Next, I bring the prayers of the people. I stand in the center of Prague, Czechoslovakia. As Jesus said to the man who was deaf, I say to the wall, 'Be opened in Jesus' name.' So we can know this is You, Lord, let it be done within the next seven weeks."

Within a short period of time, newspapers reported the fall of governmental walls in Czechoslovakia, Hungary and Germany. On November 8 (American date) the wall came down in Hungary. On November 9 the wall came down in Czechoslovakia. The Communist wall of Germany fell. Powerful prophetic words were prayed and released over these nations. Nations were changed by the prophetic voice that was released by God's prophetic people.[1]

My friend Jay Swallow has been used in powerful ways to bring change to territories. Jay is a Native American, and he has gained great favor with the leaders on some of the American Indian reservations. They know he loves the people. They also know that he loves God and carries great spiritual authority over the strongholds of the enemy. Sometimes Jay is called to come and help in situations that the local leaders are not able to handle.

Several years ago, Jay was invited to a reservation called Standing Rock. There had been an unusual number of teenage suicides on the reservation. Parents in that area lived in fear. They did not know if they would wake up the next morning and find their child dead. There was no pattern for the suicides. Educational background did not matter. Financial status made no difference. It was impossible to explain why the suicides were occurring. In a desperate attempt to find an answer, the leaders of that reservation asked Jay to come.

Late one night, Jay went to a high place on the reservation along with a few leaders and intercessors. After praying, Jay raised his voice and spoke prophetically to the reservation. "In the name of Jesus, I command the principality of suicide to come down over Standing Rock! I say that suicides stop, now!" Principalities are evil spiritual powers that rule over certain territories.

From that night forward, for the next several years, there was not one single suicide at Standing Rock! The principality of suicide had ruled there for years. A prophetic voice was needed to remove its power.

Redemptive Prophetic Promises

George Otis Jr. wrote a powerful book that helps us understand spiritual darkness over territories. He believes that there are several reasons why certain areas are affected by spiritual darkness generation after generation. He gives four possible explanations in his book *The Twilight Labyrinth*:

- Religious festivals and pilgrimages
- Cultural traditions (especially initiation rites and ancestor worship)
- Adaptive deceptions (or syncretism, that is, the fusion of different systems of thought or belief especially in religion or philosophy)
- Unresolved social injustices

"History has shown that any one of these practices is capable of maintaining a climate of spiritual oppression and despair, and their combined potency is nearly irresistible."[2]

The enemy will use whatever form he can to keep people in darkness. But God has a promise for territories and nations that have been captured by dark evil spirits. It is this: Spiritual oppression and darkness is not God's plan! God has a plan for freedom, and it includes redemptive prophetic promises that speak of restoration from the destructive plans of the enemy.

Cleansing the Land

Although God has good plans for these areas, often the land has been defiled through idolatry, bloodshed, broken covenants or immorality. The land is cleansed as these sins are repented of. It does not matter how long it has been since the sin was committed. Time does not wash away sin. Only repentance and the blood of Jesus have the power to break the hold of sin and cleanse the land.

Believers rely upon the authority of the finished work of Jesus as they repent and pray for their land. Christians have been given the authority to break the power of evil spirits. Understanding authority in intercession is critical to understanding how prophetic praying is effective. In my book *Praying With Authority*, I describe how to shift from individual authority in intercession to corporate territorial authority. I also write about the authority needed to cancel the effects of past sins over land and territories.

> Evil spirits find entrance into cities and regions in the same way they find entrance into individual lives. Demonic spirits enter territories through past sins and current sins or through generational curses and iniquities. They enter through practices of idolatry, witchcraft, victimization and trauma. Demonization of a territory results in suffering, poverty, broken relationships, sickness, disease and other maladies.[3]

These maladies are obviously not the blessing of the Lord for a land or territory. Prophets and intercessors must fight for the fulfillment of God's prophetic promises.

Understanding God's Timing

Timing is very important in this fight. Daniel the prophet understood this aspect of redemptive prophecy. The people of God were living in Babylonian captivity. God had promises of blessing for the nation of Israel when they lived in obedience to God. Due to their rebellion toward God and His prophetic word, they were exiled from their homeland.

When Daniel read the prophecy given to Jeremiah years earlier (see Daniel 9) he understood that Israel would be released from captivity after seventy years. He realized that the time for Israel's release was imminent.

> "Thus says the LORD, 'When seventy years have been completed for Babylon, I will visit you and fulfill My good word to you, to bring you back to this place. For I know the plans that I have for you,' declares the LORD,

'plans for welfare and not for calamity to give you a future and a hope.'"

Jeremiah 29:10–11

Entering Intercession

Daniel also understood that the will of God is not automatic; there is usually a spiritual battle to see the prophetic promise be made manifest. His nation's future was at stake. As a prophet, he needed to be alert and fight for the redemptive prophetic promise. So Daniel entered a time of fasting and praying.

The Old Testament books of Ezra and Nehemiah record the story of the return of the Jewish exiles from Babylon to Jerusalem to rebuild and restore their homeland. God used Cyrus, a Persian king, to shift His people into their prophetic destiny. Although Cyrus did not serve the Lord, he had a generous heart.

> In the first year of Cyrus king of Persia, in order to fulfill the word of the LORD by the mouth of Jeremiah, the LORD stirred up the spirit of Cyrus king of Persia, so that he sent a proclamation throughout all his kingdom, and also put it in writing, saying: "Thus says Cyrus king of Persia, 'The LORD, the God of heaven, has given me all the kingdoms of the earth and He has appointed me to build Him a house in Jerusalem, which is in Judah. Whoever there is among you of all His people, may his God be with him! Let him go up to Jerusalem which is in Judah and rebuild the house of the LORD, the God of Israel; He is the God who is in Jerusalem.'"
>
> *Ezra 1:1–3*

For seventy years that prophetic promise of God had been held in the atmosphere! Throughout the devastation of Jerusalem, the captivity in Babylon and the endless nights of oppression and difficulty, the word of the Lord was not negated. God waited for His time and the intercession of His people to bring His word to pass. People like Daniel understood the faithfulness of God. They remembered the prophetic promise made by God through His prophet Jeremiah and fought for it to come true.

Like prophets of old, we must understand the timing and need for intercessory prayer for the word of the Lord to be fulfilled. Knowledge of His prophetic promises helps intercessors and leaders mobilize prayer for their territories or nations. They are able to prophesy the promises of God to the land. "O land, land, land, hear the word of the LORD!" (Jeremiah 22:29). They are also able to fight with the redemptive prophetic promises that have been released over their territories in the past.

Redemptive promises are God's promises for restoration. His original plan for territories and nations is that these places receive His blessings. Although the people in these lands may have abandoned God's plan, and the land has been defiled through evil practices, God is able to redeem.

He may have spoken prophetic promises over your territory in the past. He has a plan for redeeming the land through repentance, prayer and declaring those prophetic promises. He desires to redeem the land and release His blessings.

Nations Can Be Transformed

When redemptive prophetic promises come into being, transformation occurs. Nations and territories today need to be transformed. They need to be cleansed from evil influences of alcohol, drugs, crime, disease, poverty and numerous other ills. They need the goodness of the Lord to permeate the atmosphere. It does not matter how difficult the conditions have been. It is not too hard for God to bring transformation.

God has put resources in every nation so that the people can be blessed, but corruption, greed and abuse hinder the blessings of God from flowing. Prophetic intercessors have the ability to expose the works of darkness and release the power of God.

A prophetic leader in a certain area in Texas realized that Freemasonry was deeply rooted in her region. She and another prayer leader had helped individuals be delivered from generational Freemasonry curses, and discussed following the same pattern on behalf of the land.

One component for deliverance is to reverse prophetic symbols and signs performed during Masonic inductions. Following that pattern for individual deliverance from Freemasonry, those leaders and other seasoned intercessors prayed for the region. They reversed the prophetic signs used in Masonic inductions, and with direction from the Holy Spirit carried out several prayers and prophetic acts. They repeated the words the Lord had given them as instruction: "You will line up with the Lord's standards and plumb line or you cannot stand as you are."

The following year these intercessors in Texas witnessed amazing things. Problems in the justice system in their area were exposed and changed. Their county and city governments began to change hiring practices, and implemented pay scales that were fair to all. The hidden structure of occult worship within Freemasonry that had bound the land could not hide any longer.

More and more, as leaders learn about the changes that occur because of prayer and prophetic acts, transformation happens. Reports continue to be released from cities and territories around the world that have seen transformation. The Sentinel Group, based in Lynnwood, Washington, has produced several videos that record the phenomenal breakthroughs in various cities.[4] These areas were radically changed due to the power of God through His Church in those areas.

Alistair Petrie writes about the blessings of transformation.

> Community transformation, therefore, is not only possible, but a characteristic of God's delight. As relationships between people and God and between people and people are dealt with, and as the fallen stewardship that has taken place on the land is removed and cleansed, then the eyes of the people in the land can be opened to the Gospel. The healing of the land results in people's responding to the Gospel and the presence of God dwelling in their midst. The promise is a new heart, a new spirit, a new people.[5]

My friend Carmen, who lives in Romania, is the pastor of a new church. She talks freely about how the people had lived in poverty under oppressive Communist rule. They had to work very hard with little reward during those years. They were so tired and so poor they did not have the energy or resources to fight politically.

Carmen was eager to learn about God's plans for transforming nations. She recently was able to participate in my webcast on reformation. While watching the teaching sessions, she remembered how her church prayed when they were under Communist rule. They understood that God had a redemptive prophetic promise for their nation. As they spent considerable time praying, joined by prayers of Christians all over the world, the evil regime was removed. The nation was set free.

Carmen is now eager to remind the people in her country of what life was like during those difficult years. She works to mobilize intercessors to pray and continue to fight for God's prophetic promises for her nation.

Your Area Has Prophetic Promises

Does your nation or territory or city need change? Like the individuals in these stories, you can see transformation come, too. God has good prophetic promises for your land. It does not matter about the evil forces in your area. God is more powerful than the enemy. He has plans for good and not for evil. He has a hope and good future for you and your descendants.

Fight for the prophetic promises over your territory. They are waiting to be released!

The next chapter will stir up and release a fighting spirit in you. Your future is waiting for you. Are you ready to receive all that the Lord has prophetically promised for you? Don't miss your prophetic destiny. Read on and receive the best that the Lord has for you.

Prayer

Thank You, Lord, for Your prophetic promises for my territory. I believe that You have a good future for the people who live in my land. I ask You to connect me with other prophetic intercessors. Give us revelation on how to break the evil powers that keep people in captivity. Open our eyes to see the good plans You have for us.

Help me, Lord, to stay focused on the prophetic promises You have for this area. I renounce any unbelief or doubt in my mind. I choose to believe Your word that has been released over this area. Thank You, Lord, for releasing Your power to bring change into this territory. Help me not stop praying until I see this area transformed into all You promised for us. In Jesus' name I pray, Amen.

For Further Reflection

1. What are some of the steps involved when releasing prophecy over a nation or territory?

2. Why is it important to cleanse the land for God's blessings to be released in a territory?
3. What are redemptive prophetic promises?
4. Why are timing and intercession important for the fulfillment of God's prophetic promise?
5. What does transformation in a city or region look like? Is it possible in your territory? Why?

12

THE FIGHTING SPIRIT

Champions are not made in the ring. They are merely recognized there! That statement grabbed my attention a few years ago. Boxing champions spend years in training. They strain to develop strength in their muscles. They work hard to learn coordination. They enlist help in overcoming any mindset that keeps them from winning. They also practice skills that help them to finish their punches in such a way that they can win.

The combination of many skills is what makes them champions. They are in the sport to win. They do not wait until they are in the boxing ring to develop winning skills. Their fighting spirit energizes them while they press through all the difficult training sessions.

You and I are in a similar situation. We must fight to grow and mature in prophetic ministry. We must fight to see our prophetic promises—those words given by God to us and to our land—come to pass. We may not see the manifestations overnight. It often takes time to develop prophetic sensitivity and see the fight to the finish.

But here is a revelation we can claim with confidence: We are champions. We have a fighting spirit.

A Kingdom Mindset

God put us on the earth for His purposes. Too often people only consider what they want from life. They are self-centered and focused on what makes them happy. We are not here to do what I call "breathing in and breathing out." In other words, we are not on Planet Earth merely to take up space. We are here to fulfill God's Kingdom purposes. Prophetic promises are part of His Kingdom plans for the earth. Once a person realizes that the prophetic promises of God are about His plans, it is easier to fight for them.

The Old Testament tells us of Joshua, a warrior. He was used by God to bring Israel out of the wilderness and into the land of promise. God gave him a prophetic promise that carried him into battle: "The LORD said to Joshua, 'This day I will begin to exalt you in the sight of all Israel, that they may know that just as I have been with Moses, I will be with you'" (Joshua 3:7). The promise of God's power and protection over Joshua's life was the kingdom mindset he needed. He was about to enter battles with many enemies. He needed God's prophetic promise of victory in order to fight.

The promise was not merely about Joshua and God's love for him; he was not looking for "warm fuzzy feelings." The promise was given to help him be filled with a mindset for God's purposes. Only with this kingdom mindset could he fight for God's promises in times of danger.

The Kingdom of God is not just for the future. It is available for us today. When Jesus was on the earth, He preached about the Kingdom of God. After His death and resurrection, He ascended into heaven. After He was enthroned, His Kingdom was established. The Kingdom is actually the reign of Jesus. Where He reigns, His Kingdom is made manifest and changes the earth.

The Kingdom is now growing and increasing in the earth. You and I are here to participate with God's Kingdom expansion. Any mindset that is contrary to God's Kingdom must be defeated. Only then can we fight for the promises of the Lord.

Receiving the Finishing Anointing

Many people make resolutions at the beginning of each year to accomplish something. They resolve to complete a goal for weight loss. They promise to complete a new course of study. They determine to read the entire Bible during the year. These goals are good. The challenge comes in finishing well what they have started.

We hear too many stories of Christians who do not finish well. One person who did not finish well was a well-known pastor of a very large congregation. Under his leadership the church had gained international attention for its liturgical arts, including dance and drama, as well as cutting-edge social ministry.

Then the pastor was accused of sexual misconduct, including allegations that he had molested children. DNA results proved that the young man known as his nephew was actually his son. The pastor pleaded guilty to the charges and was sentenced to ten years' probation plus a fine.

The pastor died from cancer at the age of 81. His life had remained tarnished by lawsuits and reports of sexual transgressions. How tragic for a person who began such a powerful and influential work of ministry! He started well but did not finish well.

Stories like this are always disappointing. We can become confused by the tainted lives of those exhibiting such strong spiritual gifts. Yet, we should not focus on the failures of these men and women. We should be encouraged by the lives of the thousands of gifted men and women who ran their race well. They kept their eyes on the Lord Jesus. They lived their lives to bring glory to their King. They fought a good fight of faith. They left a legacy for those who would follow them.

Gordon Lindsay is a man who finished well. Gordon was a key figure in the great revival between 1948 and 1967. During that time there was a spiritual awakening that caused a generation to experience the mighty power of the Holy Spirit through signs, wonders, miracles and healing. He was also the founder of Christ For The Nations Institute, a Bible school in Dallas, Texas.

Worship was sweet while Gordon sat on the platform Sunday afternoon, April 1, 1973. He leaned over and spoke a few words to his wife, Freda, and joined in the worship service. Sitting in his chair, Gordon sang along with the others, "Jesus, Jesus, Jesus / There's just something about that Name." Suddenly—in a moment—Gordon met the One he was singing about. He went from earth to heaven while worshiping the Lord.

Nations and generations continue to experience the fruit of Gordon Lindsay's life. He was a man who finished his race well! If people like Gordon Lindsay can finish their race well, you can, too. Run your race and fight the fight of faith to win!

We need God's supernatural grace to fight for our prophetic promises until they are made manifest. Our motto must be *Don't stop. Don't quit. Don't give up.* The Lord is always willing to help us, and He will give us what I call a "Finishing Anointing." The Greek word for *finish* is *teleo*. This is a word that means "to complete something." It means to make an end or to accomplish or finish something. This anointing is an ability to complete assignments from the Lord.

Jesus Had the Finishing Anointing

Jesus is the best example of someone who finished all that the Father gave Him to do. His purpose in the earth had been prophesied from the beginning. After the Fall, God spoke to the enemy and told him how Jesus would bruise his head, destroying the headship and authority of Satan. "I will put enmity between you and the woman, and between your seed and her seed; He shall bruise you on the head, and you shall bruise him on the heel" (Genesis 3:15).

About four thousand years later, Jesus fought for the fulfillment of that prophetic promise. He had the Finishing Anointing that caused God's purpose to be made manifest in the earth. "Therefore when Jesus had received the sour wine, He said, 'It is finished!' And He bowed His head and gave up His spirit" (John 19:30).

The Apostle Paul Had a Finishing Anointing

The apostle Paul had the ability to finish the prophetic assignment that God gave him. "I do not consider my life of any account as dear to myself, so that I may finish my course and the ministry which I received from the Lord Jesus, to testify solemnly of the gospel of the grace of God" (Acts 20:24).

Paul had a desire to be faithful to the work given to him by the Lord Jesus. He also had a desire to complete the work that he was sent to do among God's people. To complete his God-given assignments, Paul needed the Finishing Anointing.

You and I need the same anointing for our lives as we fight to see our prophetic promises become reality.

The Finishing Anointing Wins the Prize

The Bible compares all of us who are determined to win to athletes who compete in games for a prize. "Do you not know that those who run in a race all run, but only one receives the prize? Run in such a way that you may win" (1 Corinthians 9:24).

This Scripture gives us a picture of our goals. The athlete could not merely run in a race; he must run to win. The idea is of an athlete who gained the prize through strenuous exerting and eager grasping. Athletes who win have several characteristics.

A Healthful Diet

Athletes who win prizes adhere to a healthful diet. That means they cannot eat a lot of junk food. Hamburgers and milk shakes each day will not nourish their bodies for the task at hand.

I recently realized that I cannot be at my best unless I eat the food that my body requires. I understood that if I were going to finish my assignment from the Lord, it would be to my advantage to have a healthy body. I could not wait for a heart attack, diabetes or some other malady to force me to make a change in my diet. Although I have never eaten a lot of fast food, I could not use that as an excuse. I was not obese but needed to get rid of some extra weight. After several months of an adjusted diet and some counseling with a health clinic, I reached my goal. To help encourage others, the clinic even put my picture in several local newspapers!

Spiritually, we must do the same thing. We need a diet of God's promises. We must chew on these promises, meditate on them, allow them to digest.

The prophet Ezekiel was told by God to eat His word that was like a scroll. "He said to me, 'Son of man, feed your stomach and fill your body with this scroll which I am giving you.' Then I ate it, and it was sweet as honey in my mouth" (Ezekiel 3:3). The prophet was eating the words of the Lord. He would later speak those prophetic words out loud.

As we meditate on God's promises, we are eating His Word. We then speak those words out loud in intercession, proclamations and decrees. We need a strict diet of God's words rather than words of doubt and defeat. This diet nourishes us so that we can fight to the finish and not give up along the way.

Enduring Hardships

Athletes also have an ability to endure hardship. They do not stop when faced with difficult circumstances. They hold on to the promise of victory as they fight to see the fulfillment of their goal.

My friend Barbara Yoder is a spiritual athlete who has learned to endure hardships. Her husband, Paul, died several years ago. Barbara and Paul were pastors of Shekinah Christian Church, a growing church in Ann Arbor, Michigan. God made promises for the church, telling them they were destined to affect their area and the nations of the world. In the midst of those prophetic promises, Paul suddenly went to heaven.

Barbara faced several challenges. She had to determine that the promises of God were true. Could she still believe them when Paul, her husband and her companion in ministry, was not there to help? She had to endure her own times of grief and loss. On Sundays she had to endure by rising up and encouraging the congregation that had just lost one of its pastors. She wrote a book to help others endure hardships as they fight for their prophetic promises.

> God gives a prophetic word to you so that you will know where you are headed—and so that you can develop the persistence you need to press through the dark night that lies between where you are now and where you will be eventually. He wants you to press in, labor hard and work to enter into the promise. . . .

In the end, traversing the darkness will be worth it. With the fulfillment of God's promise and with rest comes joy. You will have made it through all of the temptation, through the dark night of doubts and the potential for unbelief. The break of day will be the time to celebrate. The work of your hard night will be finished.[1]

Training with the Right People

Athletes often have coaches and trainers who can help them with their techniques and encourage them to keep going.

The Bible says that just as "iron sharpens iron, so one man sharpens another" (Proverbs 27:17). Sometimes to win a battle, it helps to be connected with others who have the mindset of a warrior. We need those around us who will go to battle with us.

A friend of mine recently had a stroke. Janice is a powerful intercessor who understands spiritual battles. God had made prophetic promises to her that had not yet been fulfilled. When she had the stroke, other warriors gathered around her. They battled against the plans of the enemy. They called on the covenant promises of the Lord. They decreed that God's prophetic promises would be fulfilled in Janice's life. "Lord, we bring Janice before Your throne. We call on the power of Your covenant promises for her life. We command the bleeding to stop! We break every assignment of death and destruction from Janice's life. Thank You, Lord, that Janice will fulfill her prophetic promises. We declare total restoration for her life."

The bleeding in her brain stopped. Her blood pressure came within normal limits. Today, Janice is totally restored. In Janice's moment of crisis, she needed those with a warrior spirit to fight with her. Strong prophetic people always have an ability to fight spiritual battles.

We must know whom we can go to war with in times like this. Not everyone has a mindset to fight. Some people will run in fear in the midst of a crisis. It is okay to have lunch with these people. It is okay to be friends with them. You need to know, however, whom you can go to war with. Without the mindset of a warrior, a person is unable to fight for the victory of God's prophetic promises.

Believe You Can Win

When you learn to receive, test and release prophetic words, you win. When you grow in prophetic ministry, you win. When you stay in the fight and hold on to your prophetic promises in the midst of difficulties and setbacks, you win.

The Lord began His good work in you. He gave you prophetic promises concerning your future, and He has not changed His mind. "I am confident of this very thing, that He who began a good work in you will perfect it until the day of Christ Jesus" (Philippians 1:6). God is going to finish His work in you. That means you have the Finishing Anointing for your life.

Stay in the fight for your prophetic promises. The victory is yours.

Prayer

Thank You, Lord, for the Finishing Anointing. My desire is to finish the battle in victory. I want to see the fulfillment of Your prophetic promises in my life. Give me the grace to press through every difficult place. Help me recognize mindsets that are designed to keep me from Your promises. I reject all doubts, fears and limitations. I refuse a victim mentality. I choose a victorious, overcoming mentality.

I agree with the promises You have made to me. I will not stop. I will not quit. I receive the Finishing Anointing so that I can bring glory to Your name. Thank You, Lord, for finishing in me what You started. I will run this race so that I win and obtain my prophetic promise. In Jesus' name I pray, Amen.

For Further Reflection

1. Why is the mind the greatest battlefield?
2. How are our minds transformed?
3. Why do we need other warriors to help us battle for our prophetic promises?
4. Describe a diet of God's promises. How do you "eat the scroll"?
5. Who is someone you remember who did not finish well? What happened?
6. Have you received your Finishing Anointing?

NOTES

Chapter 1: Fighting to Hear the Voice of the Lord

1. Ernest B. Gentile, *Your Sons and Daughters Shall Prophesy* (Grand Rapids, Mich.: Chosen, 1999), 287.
2. Chuck Pierce, *When God Speaks* (Colorado Springs: Wagner, 2003), 5.

Chapter 2: Fighting to Establish Prophetic Doctrine

1. Mike Bickle, *Growing in the Prophetic* (Lake Mary, Fla.: Creation House, 1996), 99.
2. Gentile, *Your Sons and Daughters*, 233–238.
3. Barbara Wentroble, *Removing the Veil of Deception* (Grand Rapids, Mich.: Chosen, 2009), 58.
4. Bill Hamon, *Prophets, Pitfalls and Principles* (Shippensburg, Penn.: Destiny Image, 1991), 83–84.

Chapter 3: Fighting by the Means of Prophetic Prayer

1. James B. Jordan, *Through New Eyes* (Brentwood, Tenn.: Wolgemuth & Hyatt, 1988), 140.

Chapter 4: Fighting through Prophetic Dreams and Visions

1. Kevin J. Conner, *Interpreting the Symbols and Types* (Portland, Ore.: City Bible, 1992), v.
2. Jane Hamon, *Dreams and Visions* (Ventura, Calif.: Regal, 2000), 107.
3. Herman Riffel, *Your Dreams: God's Neglected Gift* (New York: Ballantine, 1985), 86.
4. Barbie Breathitt, *Dream Encounters* (North Richland Hills, Tex.: Barbie Breathitt, 2009), 61.

Chapter 5: Fighting to Establish Prophetic Sensitivity

1. Larry Kreider, *Authentic Spiritual Mentoring* (Ventura, Calif.: Regal, 2008), 16–17.

Chapter 6: Fighting for the Young Prophetic Generation

1. Cindy Jacobs, *Deliver Us From Evil* (Ventura, Calif.: Regal, 2001), 45.
2. Dayna Curry and Heather Mercer with Stacy Mattingly, *Prisoners of Hope* (New York and Colorado Springs: co-published by WaterBrook and Doubleday, 2002), 20–21.
3. Mike Huckabee, *A Simple Christmas* (New York: Penguin, 2009), 142.

Chapter 7: Fighting to Release Your Prophetic Gift

1. Chuck D. Pierce and Rebecca Wagner Sytsema, *When God Speaks* (Colorado Springs: Wagner, 2003), 22.
2. Gentile, *Your Sons and Daughters*, 20–21.
3. Chuck Pierce, *Redeeming the Time* (Lake Mary, Fla.: Creation House, 2009), 122–123.

Chapter 8: Fighting to Develop Your Prophetic Gift

1. Bill Hamon, *Prophets, Pitfalls, and Principles*, 156.

Chapter 9: Fighting to Grow in the Office of Prophet

1. Bill Hamon, *Prophets and Personal Prophecy* (Shippensburg, Penn.: Destiny Image, 2010), 62.
2. Bill Hamon, *Prophets, Pitfalls and Principles*, 10.
3. Chuck Pierce, *The Best Is Yet Ahead* (Colorado Springs: Wagner, 2001), 40.

Chapter 10: Fighting to Release Prophecy in the Marketplace

1. Os Hillman, *Faith & Work: Do They Mix?* (Alpharetta, Ga.: Aslan Group, 2000), 10.
2. Barbara Wentroble, *Prophetic Intercession* (Ventura, Calif.: Regal, 1999), 81–83.
3. Hillman, *Faith & Work*, 66.

Chapter 11: Fighting for Prophetic Fulfillment in Territories and Nations

1. Barbara Wentroble, *Prophetic Intercession* (Ventura, Calif.: Renew, 1999), 67–68.
2. George Otis Jr., *The Twilight Labyrinth* (Grand Rapids, Mich.: Chosen, 1997), 201.
3. Barbara Wentroble, *Praying with Authority* (Ventura, Calif.: Regal, 2003), 100.
4. *Transformations* video (Lynnwood, Wash.: Sentinel, 1998).
5. Alistair Petrie, *Releasing Heaven on Earth* (Grand Rapids, Mich.: Chosen, 2000), 235.

Chapter 12: The Fighting Spirit

1. Barbara Yoder, *The Overcomer's Anointing* (Grand Rapids, Mich.: Chosen, 2009), 105–106.

INDEX